CHAPTER 1

INTRODUCTION

There is risk in seeking Self-Awareness. To truly challenge ourselves and grow, we need to be open to taking in a full range of feedback, all the way from where we are doing great to where we may be failing or not meeting the others' expectations.

An open mindset is the special ingredient, the energy that will help a person find the necessary answers, apply them, and achieve the results that he or she is looking for. Some people call this their mindset; others call it their philosophy, but whatever label you attach to it, it is by all means the ingredient that will change the way you think. Your open mindset is what you learn from your friends, parents, television, it is something you need to hold onto because it will most definitely have an impact on what you do.

An open mindset can be developed and nurtured within high-trust environments, where individuals can trust that the feedback they are receiving is being offered with the best intentions for their development.

A positive philosophy turns into a positive attitude, which turns in to positive actions, which turn into positive results, which turn into a positive lifestyle."

-Jeff Olson - Author of "The Slight Edge"

How Changing Your Mindset Can Change Your Life

If you have been struggling to lose weight, improve a relationship, find a new job or just have more fun, the answer to your problems may be in your mindset. Mindset is a concept developed over a decade ago by Stanford University psychologist Carol Dweck. In her research, the psychologist tried to understand how people cope with failures. Dweck defines mindset as the view we adopt of ourselves, and proved that it can profoundly affect how we live our lives. She found that people generally fall into two categories – those with a fixed mindset and those with a growth mindset. A "fixed" mindset suggests that our intelligence, ability and personality are carved in stone and do not change much over our lifetime. An example of this mindset might be "I am not athletic" or "I am a math person", which suggest that these traits can't change. The downside to a "fixed" mindset is that these kinds of beliefs limit personal growth. By contrast, a "growth" mindset suggests that individuals have basic abilities, but can develop and cultivate these along with other traits and talents through effort and diverse strategies. This view allows one's potential to grow and opens us to greater possibilities and success. Adopting a growth mindset can improve all areas of life, from personal to professional.

OPEN MINDSET

THE STEP BY STEP GUIDE
TO IMPROVING YOUR MINDSET,
TRUSTING YOUR ABILITIES AND
DEVELOPING EXCELLENT HABITS
FOR SUCCESS

STEVEN McRYAN

Copyright © 2019 All rights reserved.

This document is geared towards providing exact and reliable information in regards to the topic and issue covered. The publication is sold with the idea that the publisher is not required to render accounting, officially permitted, or otherwise, qualified services. If advice is necessary, legal or professional, a practiced individual in the profession should be ordered.

Hence, no part of this book may be reproduced, stored in a retrieval system, or transmitted in any form or by any means, electronic, mechanical, photocopying, recording, scanning, or otherwise, without the prior written permission of the publisher.

The information provided herein is stated to be truthful and consistent, in that any liability, in terms of inattention or otherwise, by any usage or abuse of any policies, processes, or directions contained within is the solitary and utter responsibility of the recipient reader. Under no circumstances will any legal responsibility or blame be held against the publisher for any reparation, damages, or monetary loss due to the information herein, either directly or indirectly.

TABLE OF CONTENTS

CHAPTER 1 : INTRODUCTION 1

HOW CHANGING YOUR MINDSET CAN CHANGE YOUR LIFE 2

MINDSET | THE INCIDENT OF A PERSON'S PHILOSOPHY OF LIFE ... 5

CHAPTER 2 : THE MINDSETS 9

WHY MINDSETS MATTER 11

THE BASIC MINDSETS IN PRACTICE 14

WHO DO YOU WANT TO BE AND WHAT KIND OF WORLD DO YOU WANT TO CREATE? 16

A POSITIVE MINDSET - HOW TO DEVELOP ONE AND REMOVE NEGATIVITY 16

CHAPTER 3 : THE SCIENCE OF THE GROWTH MINDSET 23

COMPARING THE TWO MINDSETS 25

WHAT CAN AN OPEN MINDSET ACTUALLY DO FOR YOU? 27

THE SCIENCE OF LEARNING 29

A CLOSER LOOK AT MINDSET SCIENCE 34

CHAPTER 4 : DEVELOPING YOUR OPEN MINDSET .. 36

OVERCOMING MINDSET CHALLENGES 37

HOW TO DEVELOP A GROWTH MINDSET 38

HOW DEVELOPING MINDSETS IMPACT THE WORKPLACE 43

CHAPTER 5 : CHANGING LIFE THROUGH A GROWTH MINDSET 47

A Growth Mindset Will Change Your Life 49

Awareness of Growth Mindset 52

The Growth Mindset Will Revolutionize Your Life 56

It's Not Just For Kids 57

CHAPTER 6 : THE IMPORTANCE OF CREATING A MINDSET FOR SUCCESS 64

How To Have The Mindset For Success 66

Cultivating a Success Mindset 73

Mindset is Important for the Success of Every Entrepreneur 74

5 Important Steps to Develop a Mindset For Success and Become a Client-Attraction Magnet 76

CHAPTER 7 : THE IMPORTANCE OF COMMITMENT TO ACHIEVING SUCCESS 82

Life-Changing Decisions You Must Make To Achieve Success 84

Developing a Success-Driven Mindset 85

Achieving Success With Positive Affirmations 93

Achieve Success by "Chunking it Down" 96

CHAPTER 8 : HABITS OF SUCCESSFUL PEOPLE 99

Copy Successful People 105

CHAPTER 9 : CHANGE THE WORLD THROUGH AN OPEN MINDSET FOR GOOD THINGS TO HAPPEN ... 107

Climb Mountains One Step at a Time.............................. 108

CHAPTER 10 : GROWTH MINDSET PARENTING 117

The Importance of Praise... 117

Fixed Mindset vs Growth Mindset 117

How Parents Make The Biggest Difference.................. 119

CHAPTER 11 : THE LAW OF ATTRACTION WITH CHANGING ONE'S MINDSET 130

The History Of The Law Of Attraction 130

Manifesting Your Dreams.. 135

CONCLUSION 137

Here are 7 effective ways to upgrade your mindset:.. 137

DISCLAIMER 140

Changing from a fixed mindset to a growth one can be accomplished through three steps.

Three Steps to Grow Your Mindset

According to Dweck, an open mindset is based on the belief that we can change throughout our lifetime. While changing our beliefs can prove to be challenging, the growth mindset can still be developed in small steps.

1. *Awareness of how we think:* The first step is to become aware of our behavior. When we tune into our thoughts and start to notice our reaction to challenges, criticism, and setbacks, we can notice patterns where we are stuck. Challenges, criticism and setbacks are roadblocks for someone with a fixed mindset. For example, a fixed mindset reaction to a difficult challenge is to question whether we can succeed. If we don't think we can, why would we try only to fail? For instance, the thought "I am not going to volunteer to help my boss with that project because I am not sure I have all the skills. If I fail, I will look like a fool in front of my co-workers" limits the possibility for growth. In addition, constructive criticism is taken as an affront and a typical "fixed" mindset response is to become defensive and feel like a failure. "I can't believe she told me my paper needed work. I am a horrible writer." Setbacks can turn into a a reason to give up because they reinforce our belief that we did not have the ability in the first place. "I auditioned and didn't get a part. I knew I wasn't a good singer."

2. ***Choice:*** While it is comfortable to stick to our habitual responses, growth occurs when we make choices to change our limiting beliefs. A limiting belief keeps us in a safe zone but also prevents us from growing. For example, if my limiting belief is "I can never lose weight because my parents were overweight", why try in the first place? This choice is to default to limiting thoughts. Or in the setback example of not being selected because of lack of natural ability, the response is a choice to give up because I "failed" and my ability is fixed. The growth choice requires more effort in order for us to expand our abilities or maybe change the strategy.

3. ***Challenge the belief:*** The final step is to challenge the belief as it comes up. In order to challenge beliefs, it is important to see challenges, criticism or setbacks as opportunity for growth. For instance, in the above-mentioned example of the audition, an alternative attitude would be: "Although I did not get this part, I learned about the audition process and will continue to take voice lessons because it is important to me and I enjoy it. I might not get a part the next time either, but I will keep trying new strategies. I can ask for feedback and see how I might improve." Notice the shift from focusing solely on the result to enjoying the process, to critical with an open mindset. In addition, being open to feedback helps us develop much more than seeing it as a failure. Dweck suggests incorporating the phrase "I am not there yet" instead of "I failed" to stay encouraged and keep trying. As Henry Ford said: "Whether you think you can or think you can't - you are right!"

Mindset | The incident of a person's philosophy of life

Today's scientists have discovered that people have more capacity for lifelong learning and brain development than they had ever thought. Genetically, we all start out with differences, but it is clear that with experience, training, and personal effort, anyone can achieve what they set out to succeed in. "It's not always the people who start out the smartest that end up the smartest."

A closed mind is limited, unwilling to grow and negative, while an open mindset is able to learn, grow, is ever evolving and positive. For example - you forget to set your alarm and wake up late, you get caught in a traffic jam on your way to work, and finally you find that your work computer is kaput! In such a situation, the person with a closed mind would think "The whole world's against me", and sit there doing nothing and be fed up for most, if not all of their day. By contrast, the open-minded person would think "I must check that my alarm is set before I go to sleep", "If I had got up on time, chances are that I would have avoided the traffic", "What can I do while my computer gets fixed?"; in moving on, this person would remain positive and have another great day. I hope this demonstrates the importance of your mindset. With a closed mindset, anyone is doomed to fail, especially if they're going out there on their own and starting up a new business.

Fixed Mindset

A Fixed Mindset makes people believe that traits such as intelligence or talent are fixed, set at birth. A person with a fixed mindset lets failure or success define them. Through this fixed mindset, a lot of time is spent documenting one's talents and less by working on developing them.

Those with a fixed mindset will describe themselves as either "dumb" or "smart", with no way to change this- shying away from challenges. When faced with failure or a different challenge, they will tell themselves and others that they can't do it or will make excuses to rationalise the failure (E.g. "I didn't pass the test as I was too busy doing my homework for another subject").

Overcoming a Fixed Mindset

Often, a fixed mindset is the result of years of personal experience or emotional trauma that has caused psychological pain or doubt in one's worth. The seeds are planted during childhood or adolescence and may be very difficult to overcome. As perceived disappointments mount, the negative or defeatist mindset compounds until an individual believes this perception to be reality. Achieving success and true fulfillment requires amending a fixed mindset. The process must begin with a period of intense self-evaluation.

Question deeply entrenched personal beliefs. Examine self-image and identify ways in which the subconscious mind limits success or growth. Pay attention to the inner voice that prevents progress or complicates goal-setting. For instance, an individual wishes to lose weight. If he is of a fixed mindset, his inner voice will constantly flood his subconscious with reasons why he is wasting his time - the holidays are coming and the weight will just come back, there is too much going on at work, it will require too much effort, it will never work, etc. Conquering this kind of self-defeat is crucial to obtaining success.

The next phase in the process of exploring the self is to focus on a goal. Whether it is to get a better job, be happier in one's marriage, be a better parent, or buy a bigger house, the goal should be something significant and meaningful. Once a significant goal has been established, create a path to that goal by plotting several smaller goals along the way. These mini-goals represent tangible, attainable steps that will eventually lead to the main objective. Breaking substantial goals into stages reduces the weight of achieving what is truly desired and puts success closer at hand by situating many little victories along the way. This generates a sense of encouragement that keeps an individual focused upon the process; the main goal is reached organically, without much of the trepidation and disappointment of past attempts.

The man who wants to lose weight may set a smaller goal of taking a 10-minute walk after dinner every evening for an entire week. At the end of the week, he might set a new goal of a 20-minute walk every day for the next week. Each week is another victory, and by the end of a month he's lost ten pounds. In taking these specific, manageable steps toward his main goal, he is quieting the negative inner voice that was overwhelmed by the vague idea of losing weight.

Once those negative inner voices have been quieted, it is still necessary to open oneself to the possibility of success. This is especially true for those who have long perceived themselves as unworthy or ill-equipped for achievement or fulfillment.

CHAPTER 2

THE MINDSETS

Mindsets shape the lives we lead, the actions we take and the future possibilities of the world we live in. In this primer, we provide an overview of what mindsets are, why they matter and explore a range of practices you can use to be mindful about how and why you use mindsets.

"Your beliefs become your thoughts, your thoughts become your words, your words become your actions, your actions become your habits, your habits become your values, your values become your destiny." — Mahatma Gandhi

Eight principles can be used to describe the underlying nature of mindsets:

1) **Mindsets are habits of the mind:** The word "mindset" was first used in the 1930's to mean

2) "habits of mind formed by previous experience." In simple terms, mindsets are deeply held beliefs, attitudes and assumptions we create about who we are and how the world works.

3) **Mindsets are created by experiences:** Mindsets are created from the distinctions we are able to make about our experiences. We have experiences. Based on our experiences, we make new distinctions. Based on these distinctions, we create new mindsets.

4) **Mindsets create blind spots:** Mindsets provide us with fragmented ways of looking at the world, never with complete facts of what is. We always see the world through the filter of our mindsets and our mindsets are always incomplete.

5) **Mindsets are self-deceptive:** Any attempt to shift our mindsets will be met by powerful forces. An example of these forces is our tenancy for confirmation bias; the searching for, and recalling of, information that reconfirms our pre-existing beliefs.

6) **Mindsets shape our everyday lives:** We make our mindsets, and thereafter, our mindsets make us. Our thoughts, words and actions radiate out from our mindsets like ripples on the surface of a lake. If there is something we would like to change in our lives, such as be more creative or improve our wellbeing, we must also be open to shifting our mindsets.

7) **Mindsets create our shared world:** Mindsets are a powerful leverage point for cultural and systemic change. If we want to more consciously contribute to the world we live in, for example by acting in a way that contributes to the UN global goals, the first-ever global consensus on what must be done to address inequality,

climate change, and mental health, we must also be open to shifting our mindsets.

8) ***Mindsets can be developed in complexity:*** The more developed our mindsets become, the more we unfold towards deeper levels of wisdom and effectiveness in the world. Our mindsets evolve from simple to complex, from static to dynamic, and from ego-centric to socio-centric and world-centric. Our ability to take a perspective improves, as does our capacity to embrace ambiguity and hold paradox.

9) ***Mindsets can be transcended:*** Using the power of mindfulness, we can transcend our blind spots and self-deceptive forces, examine how the habits of our mind manifest to create our lives and our world and tap our collective capacities for profound personal and societal transformation.

Why Mindsets Matter

"It is not primarily our physical selves that limit us, but rather our mindset about our physical limits." — Ellen Langer

On a personal level, examining mindsets can create subtle yet radical clicks in our mind, when suddenly, new ways of seeing, being and ultimately acting become available to us. These liberating shifts can go on to meaningfully transform our lives in surprising and fulfilling ways. Cultivating this capacity is particularly important when engaging in creative activities, or when participating in innovative processes such as human-centred design.

For some of you, this may be enough of a reason to inquire into the nature of your mindset. There is, however, a deeper reason to examine your habits of mind.

"It is not until we see our global problems as symptoms of one fundamental, deeper-rooted crisis the symptoms of our individual and shared mindset that we can begin to mount a more profound response" — Monica Sharma

We live in turbulent times. Everyone is facing increasingly urgent and deeply interrelated challenges they haven't faced before. Collectively, we are facing an ever-growing number of social and ecological crises that continue to intensify and worsen. The ultimate source of today's great challenges — the primary root cause that creates all of our crises in the first place – is also our mindsets. All of today's great global problems are consequences of reliving unexamined habits of mind.

Thus, the deeper reason to examine our mindsets is so we can mount a self-aware response to the great challenges of our day. We simply can't respond to our personal and global problems in a meaningful way unless we also learn how to examine our mindsets as an integral part of how we live our lives.

The Three Basic Mindsets

"The most important question anyone can ask is: What myth am I living?" — Carl Jung

While everyone's mindset is unique there are some common types that are useful to be aware of.

This includes the Fixed, Growth and Benefit Mindsets, which reflect common beliefs people hold about the nature of learning and leadership.

A Fixed Mindset is symbolised by the everyday expert

"In a Fixed Mindset, people believe their basic abilities, their intelligence, their talents, are fixed traits. They have a certain amount and that's that, and then their goal becomes to look smart all the time and never look dumb." — Carol Dweck

A Growth Mindset is symbolised by the everyday learner

"In a Open Mindset people understand that their talents and abilities can be developed through effort and persistence. They don't necessarily think everyone's the same or anyone can be Einstein, but they believe everyone can get smarter if they work at it." — Carol Dweck

A Benefit Mindset is symbolised by the everyday leader

In a Benefit Mindset we not only seek to fulfill our potential, but choose to do it in a way that contributes to the wellbeing of others and society as a whole. We question "why" we do what we do, and believe in doing good things for good reasons.

For a more detailed summary of the research behind each of these mindsets please refer to our academic paper.

The Basic Mindsets In Practice

Let's say you went shopping to buy some food for dinner. If you did your shopping on autopilot, drawing on your habitual patterns of behaviour and bought what you normally would, that's an example of a Fixed Mindset.

If instead you went shopping and considered making something new and different, and bought ingredients in a mindful fashion, that's an example of a Growth Mindset. However, if you went shopping, considered making something new and also considered the wellbeing of your community and the planet, choosing socially and environmentally innovative options, that's an example of a Benefit Mindset.

This is a simple example of how the mindset we adopt shapes our everyday actions and the future possibilities of our world.

More consciously choosing your mindset

"We are called to be architects of the future, not its victims." — Buckminster Fuller

How can we become more conscious of the mindsets we are living? There is a wide range of practices for making more conscious choices, so here are a few worth noting:

- ✓ On a personal level, the practice of mindfulness helps us become more aware of how our mindsets are manifesting in our lives and our world.

- ✓ In a community setting, "Walk Out Walk On" by Margret Wheatley & Deborah Frieze provides a rich variety of practices communities are using to live the future now. Communities who come together to walk out of their limiting beliefs, attitudes and assumptions and walk on to healthy and resilient futures.

- ✓ In an organisational setting, Robert Kegan's and Lisa Laskow Lahey's concept of a Deliberately Developmental Organization is valuable for promoting the development of the whole organisation mindset.

- ✓ Otto Scharmer has developed a mindset-transcending practice called Presencing (also called Theory U). Presencing can be understood in three primary ways:

  i. Framework,
  ii. Method for leading profound change,
  iii. Way of being connected to the more authentic aspects of our self and the world.

David Gray's book, "Liminal Thinking", provides a range of nine practices for minimising reality distortion, envisioning new possibilities and creating positive change. These practices can be summarized as three simple precepts:

1. Get in touch with your ignorance.
2. Seek understanding.
3. Do something different.

Who do you want to be and what kind of world do you want to create?

"You cannot get through a single day without having an impact on the world around you. What you do makes a difference, and you have to decide what kind of difference you want to make." — Jane Goodall

In this primer, we've explored what mindsets are and why they matter; we have also provided a range of practices you can use to be mindful about how and why you use mindsets.

A Positive Mindset - How to Develop One and Remove Negativity

People suffering from mental health conditions like anxiety disorder and clinical depression commonly present negative cognitive patterns as part of their illness. These usually fade away along with recovery from an illness episode.

We can more easily avoid negativity that comes from people we only meet occasionally. But what if that 'circle of negativity' was at home or had become embedded at your work place, and you would have to face it every day? How easily can you avoid it then?

Let us begin by looking at 3 key reasons why we need to stop feeding negativity:

1. **Negativity can waste valuable time and resources:** Picture this for a moment - you go to work with the intention of completing your tasks for the day. You find your colleagues discussing about a change introduced

recently by the management. You somehow get drawn into the debate. If not mindful, you could get caught up in an endless discussion and waste your valuable time resource.

Similarly, gossiping and arguing your case for the sake of a "hard-to-please" ego not only wastes time, but also reduces productivity.

2. **A negative mindset affects your health - negatively, of course:** A negative mindset leads to an overall negative health outcome. It makes one more prone to the harmful effects of stress, releasing more stress hormones and reducing endorphins (the so-called "feel-good" hormones). Scientific evidence shows that a negative attitude can adversely affect our immune system, making us prone to infections and other physical and psychological ailments.

By comparison with people who have a positive disposition and outlook on life, individuals with a habitually negative disposition could have a higher risk of memory and mental health problems, including depression.

3. **Focusing on the negative only contributes to its power:** Negativity has a growing ground. Just like one rotten apple in the basket can spoil the rest, a dominating, firmly held negative belief can influence your thoughts and state in a way that does not serve you. Soon enough, you find yoursel becoming quite pessimistic and cynical.

You fail to communicate effectively and trivial things seem to matter more than they should, leading to pointless conflicts with others. In next to no time, you become part of the problem rather than part of the solution.

Why do we feed negativity?

Adopting a negative stance does not take much effort (although energy can get expended), whereas to think and behave in a positive way requires some persistence and commitment.

A fear of 'loss' can drive negativity. The unfulfilment of our needs, for instance a lack of loving or meaningful relationships, ill-health, ongoing stress or tiredness, can also feed negativity. We may get into a "negative state" from time to time, due to external stresses or internal conflict. Some people with past negative experiences may consciously or "sub-consciously" expect more of the same, thereby making 'negativity' a conditioned but unhealthy response.

Let me share a few ways of addressing negativity in your life:

1. *Cultivate an open and positive mindset:* People who project negativity on a consistent basis typically have low self-esteem. They feel badly about themselves, and their negativity could reflect those feelings.

Adopting an open mindset should enable you to listen non-judgmentally, practice genuine empathy, and to appreciate the others' viewpoints. You do not have to share their views or try to solve their problems for them - only encourage them to look for solutions themselves. Keep a distance from the

Open Mindset

others' negative emotions if you want to help them in a meaningful way.

Research has shown that our expectations of people can influence their behaviour and vice-versa. When we label someone as "negative", we expect them to complain, be pessimistic and focus on problems most of the time. This expectation or prediction often comes true.

Would it help to say that no such thing as a "negative person" exists, only a person with negative tendencies?

2. ***Infuse energy and enthusiasm:*** When you look after yourself well, with passion for your life, the vibrant energy will sooner or later rub off on those around you. Positive energy vibes can have a contagious effect!

3. ***Use language mindfully:*** Try repeating the following out loud (with emotion for impact):

"I feel crap"

"This food is disgusting!"

"This traffic jam is doing my head in."

"This is absolutely appalling. How dare she complain to the boss about me?"

Now try these ones instead;

"I don't feel very good."

"This food doesn't taste nice."

"This traffic jam is quite annoying."

"This does not feel right. I wonder what made her complain to the boss about me."

How we frame our sentences and the words we use on a regular basis have a big role to play in either feeding or defusing negativity. Words like "always", "never", "everything", "everybody", "nothing", "nobody", etc. can easily distort reality. So choose your words deliberately and mindfully.

1. ***Stop blaming others (and yourself):*** You need to accept that you cannot control external events and that no one can make you feel a certain way; only you can! No matter how bad the situation, no amount of blaming, cynicism or back-lashing will change it. Seek to learn and experience something positive from it, no matter what.

2. ***Positively energise your thoughts:*** Negative thoughts and accompanying emotions can wreak havoc when allowed to run their free course. Rather than resisting them, first accept their presence. Ask yourself "do they serve me and my loved ones?". Your body will send out vibes. If these make you feel uneasy, remind yourself of the consequences of holding on to these. Make a conscious decision to discard and get rid of them for good. Discarding them will create an empty space in your mind. Fill it with positive and happy thoughts, and charge these up with physical and emotional energy. This will make you feel positively energised!

3. ***Have a break:*** Mental exhaustion can challenge you from staying focused and from maintaining a positive attitude. Noises from the outside world compounded by

your own value judgements, inner dialogues and "things to do" lists can distract you.

Give your body and mind the break it deserves even if only for 5 minutes every hour or so. This will not only help you re-orient yourself to the tasks that need completion, but also enable you to put in your best efforts.

4. ***Choose healthy habits and a healthy lifestyle:*** Lead a healthy lifestyle and pay particular attention to exercising your body and mind. Among other things, practice gratefulness on a daily basis, read inspirational stories, listen to music, connect with your loved ones, devote time to your children, participate in sporting activities and reach out to help others in need.

5. ***Resourcefulness:*** Resourcefulness is a state of mind from where creative energy flows. It taps into your inner resource and aligns you with your core values. When you try hard to resist negativity, you only manifest more tension and end up in an unresourceful state. Accept its presence and do not blame yourself.

Try out ways to get into a resourceful state. Make a list of things, people or activities that evoke good feelings in you - make a note of these in your personal journal. Schedule these positive triggers in your daily routine, indulge in them and reap the benefits.

6. ***Expect 'negativity' to have a short life span:*** Remember, if you remain passive, negativity will take you for a joyless ride. It is not enough to think positively. You also need to shake off the stubborn, negative particles that you might

have collected and flush them out of your mind. Create an expectation that they will move on, and they will!

7. ***Have you addressed your needs:*** We all have needs - our physical, emotional and spiritual needs. Turn your attention to them and see which ones need addressing. Address them and you will experience freshness in life!

CHAPTER 3

THE SCIENCE OF THE GROWTH MINDSET

While no single theory covers everything, we can at least teach what we think/know makes a difference and provide both the stories and the science behind it. Both are important. The stories capture the students' imagination. Seeing other people demonstrate skills has a big impact on your belief that you can do it yourself. The science helps us back our theories up with evidence and ensures that the novices aren't being taught things like learning styles again. So, here are some growth mindset stories and the science behind them.

The idea that your mindset affects your life is hardly a new one. Many great thinkers, writers, and orators have extolled the virtues of mastering your mind to improve yourself for centuries. No, millenniums. Basically, think one way, get one result. Think another, get another.

"Your thoughts determine your reality" has been a popular refrain for ages. It sounds good and it feels right, but is it true? Michael Jordan is just one person on an endless list of anecdotal stories that would say yes. Unfortunately, anecdotes are unreliable. What we really need is science.

Something that puts a stake in the ground and explains why the anecdotes work (and how they can work for us).

Enter Carol Dweck, a professor whose soft-spoken demeanor and fragile constitution could easily conceal her profound knowledge about the way your mind works if it weren't for the fact that, when she speaks, her conviction forces you to listen. And that conviction is well earned. Her decades of research into the way we learn have built a sturdy foundation of empirical evidence that tells that yes, your mindset matters!

That evidence has led to her magnum opus, "Mindset: The New Psychology of Success". It's a fascinating read, but the crux of it is that you can measure your mindset on a continuum. At one end of the scale is a fixed mindset. At the other end is the open one.

What Dweck uncovered is that people on the right (open mindset) tend to believe their intelligence and their abilities are malleable, that they can change (aka grow) based on how much effort they put into it. They think about their brain like a muscle. If they use it more and challenge it, it will grow stronger.

By contrast, those on the left (fixed mindset) consider those things to be set traits, like their eye color or if they have dimples when they smile. If you're smart, it's because you were born that way. If you're talented, the talent comes from your genes. Not much you can do about it either way.

So that's a simple explanation of the difference between fixed and growth mindset, but why does it actually matter?

Comparing The Two Mindsets

The two mindsets start manifesting as soon as children become able to evaluate themselves, as early as at the age of four. Even at this young age, when offered the choice, children with a fixed mindset opted to redo an easy jigsaw puzzle, versus the children with a growth mindset, who enthusiastically chose a hard one after another. Let's compare the two mindsets and draw conclusions.

- **Success:** People with the fixed mindset want to make sure they succeed, because smart people should always succeed. Actually, you have to be pretty much flawless from the get-go.

  For people with the growth mindset, success is about stretching themselves. It's about becoming smarter.

- **Thriving:** People in a fixed mindset thrive when things are safely within their grasp. When things get too challenging, they lose interest, because they're not feeling smart or talented.

  People in a growth mindset thrive on challenges. The bigger the challenge, the bigger the stretch.

- **Potential:** The fixed mindset advocates subscribe to the idea that you can test and measure your ability right now, and project it into the future to understand your potential. Their growth mindset counterparts simply understand their potential as their capacity to develop their skills with effort over time. They don't know where their effort and time will take them in the future.

- **Failure:** The fixed mindset believers must succeed perfectly and immediately, because a potential failure means lack of competence and will define them as "The Person Who Didn't Get Into The X College".

  Even in the growth mindset, failure can be a painful experience, but it doesn't define you; in fact, it's an opportunity to take control, deal with the problem, and learn from it.

- **Self-Esteem:** When failing, the fixed mindset people try to repair their self-esteem, looking for people who are worse off than they are, assigning blame or making excuses.

- For the people who believe their current qualities can be developed, failing still hurts, but it also signals that their abilities can be expanded. They recognise that failure is the path to success.

- **Effort:** From the point of view of the fixed mindset, effort is only for people with deficiencies. From their point of view, if you're considered a genius, a talent, or a natural, then the effort can be reduced for two reasons:

  Great geniuses are not supposed to need effort; just needing it speaks volumes about your (in)ability.

  Effort robs you of all your excuses; without effort, you can always say, "I could have been XXXX." But once you try, you can't say that anymore.

  As far as the open mindset is concerned, doing nothing about something you want badly is almost inconceivable.

From this perspective, you can look back and say "I gave my all for the things I valued."

- **Achievements:** The fixed mindset limits achievement. These people's minds are flooded with thoughts and doubts about their efforts, which leads to inferior learning. It also turns other people into judges instead of allies.

When it comes to the open mindset, important achievements require a clear focus, all-out effort, and countless strategies to test and implement. Plus, people are allies, aiding the journey towards learning and improving.

What Can An Open Mindset Actually Do For You?

The difference between a fixed and a growth mindset is simple to understand. You tend to believe you are who you are and there's not much you can do about it (fixed), or you believe you're in control of who you are, and you can change if you try (growth). But is one actually better than the other?

According to Dweck, a growth mindset is absolutely better. In almost every way.

What she discovered through a series of experiments and studies is that people with a growth mindset not only learn more new things, but they learn those new things faster and better.

And the long-term outcomes of those findings were crystal clear, too: students with a growth mindset got better grades and ascended to higher levels of achievement later in life. They met more of their goals and stayed on more successful paths.

Why?

Because the mindset you have changes everything about how you approach challenges and opportunities, including whether you use the word "challenge" or "opportunity" for the same circumstance. In "Mindset", Dweck explains that "no matter what your ability is, effort is what ignites that ability and turns it into accomplishment."

And according to her research, a growth mindset is what motivates you to put in that effort. It's what makes you dig deep to navigate the difficulties of learning something new. When you believe you're capable of growing and overcoming obstacles, and that the process can make you smarter, stronger, or better, you feel a lot more motivation to put in the hours of difficult work that will actually get you there. You're striving for something you know you can achieve, so you're at peace with the struggle.

But when you're stuck in a fixed mindset, you're exactly that: stuck. If you can't grow, if you can't learn, if you can't change, why would you bother trying? You don't think you can do it, and failure would just confirm it. Would you try to drive your car 300 miles if you only thought you had 100 miles worth of gas in the tank?

Dweck's research shows that the students she examined were far less likely to even try to learn something new when they showed signs of a fixed mindset. And when they did try, they didn't try as hard or for as long as the ones who had a growth mindset.

Here's what Dweck said in "Mindset":

"In the fixed mindset, everything is about the outcome. If you fail or if you're not the best it's all been wasted. The growth mindset allows people to value what they're doing regardless of the outcome. They're tackling problems, charting new courses, working on important issues. Maybe they haven't found the cure for cancer, but the search was deeply meaningful."

And when you think about it, we all start our lives with an intense growth mindset. That should make it easy and natural to be an open, future-oriented person. Yet all of us – at least occasionally – struggle with a fixed mindset.

The Science of Learning

Carol Dweck found that those who are wired to learn also succeed more. And further, our brains are in a constant flux of change when we learn, something which happens throughout our lifetime. Here's what she found:

"In [my] research in collaboration with my graduate students, we have shown that what students believe about their brains, whether they see their intelligence as something that's fixed or something that can grow

and change, has profound effects on their motivation, learning, and school achievement."

Dweck goes on to describe individuals who have a fear of change and individuals who embrace and seek change as living in "different psychological worlds." In the former, change can cause devastating setbacks, while in the latter, challenges are relished and the individuals persevere in the face of change.

This is the main difference between a fixed mindset and a growth mindset. In a fixed mindset, intelligence is believed to be a given that each person has a certain amount of. That's that. In a growth mindset, however, the belief is that intelligence is ever-growing, ever-changing, a potential that can be realized through learning.

➢ **Flow:** Learning can also get you into an experience of flow. During flow, an individual is completely absorbed by an activity which involves their creative abilities. Discovered by Positive Psychologist Mihaly Csikszentmihalyi, "flow is the zone, the mental state of operation in which a person performing an activity is fully immersed in a feeling of energized focus, full involvement and enjoyment in the process of the activity."

➢ **Purpose:** Learning gives us purpose. Having a list to grow and check off gives us something to live for. This is different than being goal-oriented. When we have things to learn, we know that we are constantly evolving, and our life, skills and achievements are not static.

From a health perspective, stress and depression can take a major toll on the heart. One study involving 4,500 adults with coronary artery disease found that those who were also plagued with extreme depression and/or stress were 50% more likely to die or have a heart attack in the next 6 years. Scary stuff!

However, in another study, researchers found that having a strong sense of purpose in life actually lowers the risk of stroke and heart disease. Randy Cohen, the lead author of the study, says: "Developing and refining your sense of purpose could protect your heart health and potentially save your life."

How to Learn

This funny thing happens to adults: we forget how to learn. As kids, we are constantly in school, experiencing things for the first time and forced into daily learning situations. As adults, we are often in the same job day after day, very rarely given new tasks, and our learning muscles atrophy. I want to flip this on its head. Just because you are out of school, that doesn't mean you have to stop learning:

What: The first thing I want you to think about is what you want to learn about. This can vary all the way from skills like making sushi or changing a tire to entire topics like French or tennis. Your activities can also be related to different subjects that you are interested in, like Italian history, how wine is made, or eating vegan. Brainstorm a list of ideas and topics below:

How: You also want to think about how you best learn. Do you like reading about things? Do you like having things explained to you? Do you need to try things out yourself to understand them? Check off your favorite methods:

- ✓ Books
- ✓ Audiobooks
- ✓ In-Person Classes
- ✓ Video
- ✓ Experimenting
- ✓ By yourself
- ✓ With a learning partner
- ✓ With a learning group
- ✓ With a mentor or tutor

When: The biggest hurdle adults have to overcome when it comes to learning is fitting learning into their schedules. Many people tell me, "After a full day of work, I am just too tired to learn." Or "I don't know when I will have the time to learn a new skill." This is ok, you just have to figure out when the best learning time for you is. Here are some ideas, check off the ones that sound promising:

- ✓ Listening to an audiobook or podcast while you get ready in the morning
- ✓ Watching an online video while you cook or eat breakfast

Open Mindset

- ✓ Taking 20 minutes every day before work to do a chapter in a workbook
- ✓ Listening to an audiobook or podcast while you commute
- ✓ Taking a lunchtime class
- ✓ Doing a 30-minute exercise or skill-building session while you eat lunch
- ✓ Watching an online video while you cook or eat lunch
- ✓ Taking a class after work
- ✓ Joining a learning group once a week after work
- ✓ Meeting with a learning partner over happy hour

Where: Here are some favorite resources for learning.

- ✓ Audible: This is an amazing resource. Learn while you cook, clean, drive, relax, anywhere!
- ✓ Your local library: If you are on a budget or have no idea where to start, your local library is a fantastic resource. Go talk to your libarians to find out what classes or books they have.
- ✓ Your online library: Most libraries now have online learning systems where you can check out audiobooks, get downloads and watch videos.

A Closer Look at Mindset Science

Imagine you're invited to be part of a high-visibility special project to design something new and solve a complex problem. You would be collaborating with people you don't know so well, from different parts of the company. Some you secretly call "the rockstars". What's your gut reaction? Curiosity and excitement to try and learn something new? Hesitation and worry about whether you can ace it? Will you accept the opportunity?

Carol Dweck, Ph.D., would say that how we respond is a hint about our "mindset". Mindset is different from a particular perspective or attitude that we adopt. It runs in the background, is often trained into us in childhood, and reveals itself through our actions and reactions. It is a quick well-travelled path through our brain that triggers the belief and context based on which we see our "self".

Dweck's research identifies two mindsets: "fixed mindset", in which we believe our traits, talents, and abilities to be static; and "growth mindset", in which we believe our basic abilities and intelligence can be developed with attention and effort.

Let's go back to the initial scenario. Let's assume you said yes to the invitation; however, you didn't perform and contribute as you would have liked. What was the consequence? Did you beat yourself up, thinking and feeling that you failed to prove yourself, your smarts? Did you give yourself a pep talk about how you will prepare for the next time and engage differently? Now switch your perspective…

How do you respond to a friend or colleague who is telling you about their experience?

Dweck's research reveals a cascade of mindset consequences in motivation, behavior, feedback, interpretation and trajectory.

Bringing our mindset to the surface, understanding the triggers, and noticing the subtle ways in which it influences our decisions and actions is another way to explore the gap between where we are today and where (and how) we wish to be in all our roles in the future. Mindset brings additional self-awareness if we assume others are just like us in how they respond.

CHAPTER 4

DEVELOPING YOUR OPEN MINDSET

An open mindset can be developed throughout life. This is especially good news to people who are fifty and older, because so many of their habits have become ingrained and have turned into routine.

A mindset is an attitude or disposition that determines our responses to and interpretations of particular situations. It is shaped by our beliefs and experiences. Think of the mindset as the way we approach and deal with particular situations.

Fixed or growth?

Early research suggested that our mindsets were fixed, which contributes to the belief that our intelligence is also fixed. Recent studies carried out by Carol Dweck and others have shown that mindsets and ability are not fixed. Just as you can build up your physical muscles and become stronger, you can also develop your mental "muscles", thus becoming a better learner and thinker. Developing a growth mindset helps you do this.

Overcoming Mindset Challenges

We all have those days when we drop our heads and beat ourselves up; you might even let out a few expletive words for good measure. The steps taken to overcome mindset challenges are the following: focus on the one, take it personal, see the future, and lead the pack.

> **Hear Those "Voices":** Learning to overcome a fixed-mindset challenge begins with learning to control your emotions. Only then can you achieve optimal performance during competition. First, you need to pay attention to those negative voices; you know, the ones coming from family members that prove how much of a "failure" you are, or the ones from coaches that explain your "lack of talent". There may have even been laughter from classmates or club memberships. A mentor who would snap at you the moment you hit a setback. You may have developed a reactive "habit" - automatic response – to an emotional stimulus. Pushing those old suppressed buttons will give you a release and an understanding, but despite the good intentions that may be hidden behind them, they can also trigger an emotional upheaval, easily sweeping you away. Fortunately, there is one way to stop the spiral of uncontrollable emotional reactions - refocusing. Consciously stepping back to draw your focus back to your senses and the physical effects they may manifest: elevated heart rate, sweaty palms, nausea, tight or tense muscles, anxiety, and shallow breathing.

> **Acknowledge and Accept:** Stay in the present moment, acknowledging that these physical effects are poignant, so that you can process the information as if you were a doctor observing a patient. Comprehend your emotional arousal as an imaginary threat, and your intensified state of mental stress or physical excitement as a normal response that can be reduced by controlling your emotions. Slow down. Accept that you can help your brain learn to process new "habits" and thus effectively stay grounded; stretch and breathe, visualize or focus on energizing cues that epitomize how you want to perform or transform negative energy into positive energy.

> **Choice:** You have a choice; interpret negative challenges or setbacks from a lack-of-talent fixed mindset or from a positive, aptitude-growth mindset. When you doubt your talent, change your focus - with time and effort, believe you can learn a particular skill or achieve a goal. If you hit a setback or face criticism, keep learning and persevere.

How To Develop A Growth Mindset

- *Effort:* By focusing on the processes and effort that allow people to be successful, you give them a template to replicate next time. Praising effort has been shown to have a long lasting impact. In one study, children aged 2-3 who were praised for their effort were more likely to have a growth mindset five years later, when aged 7-8. Furthermore, this type of praise has been demonstrated to enhance people's intrinsic motivation.

- ***Different Strategies:*** In a recent interview, Dweck stated that "telling kids to try harder isn't enough to promote a growth mindset". One strategy that could work is advising them to ask metacognitive questions, such as "what could I do differently?". This helps children avoid the trap of working hard but repeating the same mistakes.

- ***Learning:*** Forty years ago, a psychologist in America studied how primary school students viewed an upcoming test. Some students viewed it as a chance to test how much they have learnt. Others viewed it as an opportunity to compare themselves against their classmates. Those who focused more on comparison are said to have an ego-orientation, whereas those who focused on learning are task-orientated. This work was the basis of some of Dweck's early research. Task orientation has since been associated with better motivation, confidence, self-regulation, academic performance and reduced anxiety. Although this is probably common sense, where possible, try to foster a mindset that is focused on learning, development and improvement, and not just on outscoring a classmate.

- Asking for Feedback: People with a growth mindset seek out and value feedback more than those with a fixed mindset. One possible reason for this is that those with an open mindset see new events as an opportunity to learn new things, develop and challenge themselves; by contrasr, those with a fixed mindset see new experiences as a test fortheir ability (and therefore associate them with judgement). Apart from giving someone feedback, the actual behaviour that should be praised is their seeking out this feedback in the first place. This will lead to them asking for feedback again in the future, which is a positive response to either success or failure.

- ***Persistence:*** The ability to persist and overcome setbacks is seen by many as a key life skill. Many Olympic champions have developed this skill, and they present it as a key part of their success. Research indicates that those with a growth mindset will persist for longer. Research in America on 'Grit' (defined as long-term perseverance and passion towards a singular goal) is in its early stages, but this characteristic has been linked to success in school, university, military training and generally in life. We think this will be an interesting area of research to keep an eye on over the coming years.

- ***Choosing Difficult Tasks:*** People with a fixed mindset equate making mistakes with having low levels of ability. This can lead to people playing it too safe for fear of looking bad. Over time, this leads to worse performance. Mistakes happen and they are inevitable. Learning is messy and never straight-forward. By encouraging someone to choose difficult tasks and challenge themselves, we will help them develop their mindset. This growth mindset can, in turn, result in a sense of courage and curiosity, important life skills that extend beyond getting good grades or playing sports better.

- ***Setting High Standards:*** In a fascinating study related to knowing one's limits, researchers asked participants to cycle as hard as they could for 4000m. Later, participants were given the same instructions, but had to race against an avatar of their previous ride. What they didn't know was that the avatar was actually going faster than their previous ride. The result? The participants rode alongside their avatar, going significantly further than during their previous attempt. The implication is that people are poor predictors of their best efforts and, when pushed, may surpass their own expectations.

5 Ways to Shift Your Mindset for Change

When you need to make a change, whether adjusting unwanted behaviors or carving a new path, having the right mindset can significantly affect your ability to succeed. A fixed mindset will be more resistant to change than a growth mindset. Being able to shift your mindset as needed is a skill that will provide you with a distinct advantage in creating desired changes, as well as increase your effectiveness in other areas of your life.

For example, have you ever needed to come up with new, brilliant ideas for a project or to solve a problem, but your mind just wasn't in a creative mode? Your mindset can have a significant impact on your impact and success.

Try these five tips to shift your mindset and create a map for successful change:

1. **Reengage both sides of your brain (right-brain and left-brain processes):** You need both logic and creativity to be at your best, and if you can't access the other, you will be limited in what you are able to accomplish. Try

centering exercises or physical exercises that re-integrate both sides of the brain (exercises that cause you to cross the midline of your body alternately left/right).

2. ***Focus on positive attributes:*** Obsessing about negative events wires the brain to look for and expect negativity. Conversely, noticing your strengths, successes, and focusing on the positive aspects of your situation invites the brain to predict further successes.

3. ***Visualize the outcome or changes you want to see happening:*** Experiments with athletes show that the brain does not differentiate between visualized practice (such as nailing a free throw) and actual practice in which you physically perform the action. The same sequence is fired in the brain when you visualize doing something as when you actually do it. Create a clear visualization of the outcome you desire as if you have already achieved it, and practice "seeing" that outcome in your mind every day.

4. ***Seek out new perspectives and insights:*** Collaborative conversations with others, where they can help you see the situation differently, help create new pathways in the brain that you can then access when you get stuck in a particular mindset.

5. ***Take specific action even before you have motivation:*** Developing a plan for what you want to change or achieve and repeatedly setting it into motion will hardwire your visualizations and insights into your brain. Action is how the visualization of the future actually becomes the present.

How Developing Mindsets Impact The Workplace

Companies are now starting to realize that the difference between fixed and growth mindsets in adults can significantly impact workplace performance. In addition to the personal development benefits, a growth mindset also makes employees better team players. The video below gives a brief overview of the concept:

With a growth mindset, people will be:

- Motivated to learn and improve with feedback
- Able to change and adapt skills, behaviors and attitudes faster
- Inspired by their teammates' achievements
- Willing to share knowledge and help others succeed

To help people in your company develop a growth mindset, ask yourself these four questions:

1. Are your performance management practices hindering growth?

Stack ranking, for example, is a performance management practice that forces managers to rank their employees from the best to the worst performing individual. Rather than encouraging high performance and growth, stack ranking pits employees against each other, creating competitive environments steeped in fixed mindset mentalities.

If you want to foster a growth mindset at the workplace, it will be important to ensure that your performance management process encourages the regular exchange of feedback, conversations with managers, and opportunities for professional development.

2. Are your people coached with a growth mindset?

You will need to take a close look at current practices within your organization, to see whether or not they encourage a growth mindset. For example, do you see teams divided into star employees and the rest? Do you hear people differentiating between their top performing team members and others? Make sure that you help people within your organization recognize when they are already applying a growth mindset. Identify the teams or departments where this is happening so that you can provide them with additional support.

Ultimately, you want team leaders to coach with a growth mindset, which will help people be more open to learning and developing new skills. Considering that nowadays the half-life of a job skill is about five years, people need to be willing to adapt and learn on a regular basis. Those with a fixed mindset are more likely to fall behind.

This doesn't mean that you should encourage people to learn dozens of new skills every year, but team leaders should be able to understand whether people are blocked due to a lack of interest or a feeling that they're simply not good enough.

3. How do your teams set goals?

According to Dweck, the way teams set goals can have an impact on their mindset. Her research shows that people with fixed mindsets are more likely to set performance goals as opposed to development goals. While this may not seem shocking, performance-related goals are more closely tied to things people are already good at. On the other hand, by setting learning goals, employees take on new challenges, experiment, and grow.

Team leaders should help people find the right balance between performance-based and development goals.

4. Is feedback helping or hurting?

It's common knowledge that recognition and giving people praise can motivate teams into high performance. However, have you taken into account how people are praising one another?

Ideally, people should share feedback based on the effort they perceive, not on their colleague's natural ability. Upon receiving feedback and to support the growth mindset, people can explain what steps they took to help them achieve this level. Meanwhile, it's important for teams to give each other constructive feedback, as there's no end to what they can learn. With regular input on their performance, people will be able to set new goals for themselves and strive for continuous improvement.

As more people within your organization embrace the growth mindset, you'll be able to come back to your feedback culture. You might even find that since people are more open to developing, they've started to request feedback more often themselves! Both a growth mindset and a culture of feedback ultimately support People Enablement, putting people in the driver's seat of their careers.

CHAPTER 5

CHANGING LIFE THROUGH A GROWTH MINDSET

When we're born, our brains are malleable and can be easily shaped by our experiences and environment. However, scientists have long believed that as we age, our neural paths begin to harden like drying cement.

You know that saying "You can't teach an old dog new tricks"? That saying has perpetuated a myth that the old dogs' brain has hardened in ways that make him unable to learn anything new. For many decades, the scientific community thought this to be true of animals and people alike. But, as science has progressed, we've found that such an idea simply does not correspond to reality.

Modern neuroscience has proven that our brains are more malleable than we could have ever imagined, even if we are already well into later stages of life. Our brain's plasticity comes as a result of groups or individual neurons forming new connections. These new connections come about when an individual has new experiences or learns something new. As you learn more, these new connections get stronger. Myelin, a fatty substance in the brain, wraps itself around new connections to insulate them. The more we practice and learn, the thicker the myelin gets and the stronger our new neuronal connections become.

We can teach an old dog new tricks. We just have to make sure that we teach him for long enough for his myelin to wrap around his new networks. This is great news for people who have a ten-year-old dog who still isn't potty trained!

Still, many of us tend to feel let down when they face the difficulties of learning new skills or mastering old ones. We blame the rapidly evolving technology, job competition or lagging energy levels for our failings. But we don't need to. All we need to do is adopt a growth mindset, and then we can learn and grow as we please.

The relevance of the growth mindset for people who are interested in positive change

With climate change, cuts to local services, refugee and homeless crises, and many other issues to solve in our modern lives, there is a pressing need to act. We need to move faster. We need to be more effective in finding innovative solutions. Just as external factors such as technology, improved data and the rise of the social entrepreneur bring changes to the sector itself, so too are the requirements facing tomorrow's social entrepreneurs changing. And change demands adaptation. We enable adaptation through a set of assumptions and attitudes we hold about ourselves, otherwise known as "mindset". And adaptation infers learning.

It's the growth mindset that removes the self-imposed limits to your capacity to learn and engage in this constantly changing landscape. We can define the growth mindset as the belief that genetics do not determine your intelligence. That intelligence is a liquid capacity, one that, like the muscles in your body, can be and is strengthened as a result of work. Like your physical prowess, your intelligence is not set in stone! Derek Sivers arrived at this rhyme (paraphrased here with apologies) that sums up the growth mindset beautifully:

A Growth Mindset Will Change Your Life

The idea of a growth mindset came from the famous Stanford researcher Carol Dweck. Dweck and her team stumbled upon the phenomenon when observing students and their various responses to failure. Why was it, they wondered, that some students could bounce back from a setback like nothing had happened, while others sulked and fumed when obstacles got in their way?

It wasn't the magnitude of the setback, nor the consequences of the setbacks that determined the student's responding behaviors; in fact, it was their mindsets. Some students had a fixed mindset, while others had a growth mindset. The ones with a fixed mindset believed that capabilities are innate and were sure that no matter how hard they tried, they wouldn't be able to do anything about their failures. The growth mindset kids believed that they could eventually learn to do anything if they put in effort and practice.

We can learn a lot about ourselves through the experiences of Dweck's students. And the most important thing is that we'd better develop our very own growth mindsets!

How to Get Your Own Growth Mindset

If you don't already have a growth mindset, there is good news: developing one isn't too hard! The real struggle comes down to alleviating the shame and embarrassment we feel when it comes to failure and setbacks.

A member of our team has a fantastic antidote for battling shame and embarrassment. His father, Randy, made the practice of embracing failure into a tradition of sorts, a practice his children carry on in their own lives. When Randy's children were small, he would share his most embarrassing setbacks with them at the dinner table and encourage his kids to share their own stories. Even today, with the kids grown and spread around the country, Randy gets them all on the same call to tell them about his latest embarrassing stories. They lovingly refer to them as "Humble Stories".

Some recent Humble Stories include:

The time he simply forgot where he had parked his rental car and had to spend a whole day scouring the city before he gave up and called the rental company to tell them the bad news.

The time he found a dead, pregnant black widow and opened her up on the kitchen counter only to find that her thousands of babies were still very much alive and scurrying to all corners of the house.

Randy's stories aren't just a bonding experience for the family, they are an opportunity to share an incredibly powerful message: we all screw up, we all make mistakes. Be vulnerable, laugh it off and keep going! By demonstrating to his children that it is okay to fail and be embarrassed, they've all gone on to develop a very strong growth mindset, and are empowered to achieve whatever they set their hearts on.

To develop a growth mindset, we should all try to be a little like Randy.

1. First, we should acknowledge our setbacks or unfavorable circumstances. We don't want to call them failures, though. We want to call them learning opportunities. Marvel at the processes more than the results. Jackie Joyner-Kersee, a track and field athlete and Olympic gold medalist once said, "I derive just as much happiness from the process as from the results. I don't mind losing as long as I see improvement… If I lose, I just go back to the track and work some more." Learn to think more like Joyner-Kersee and enjoy the process instead of simply focusing on the outcomes.

2. Now we want to acknowledge any shame that might accompany those learning opportunities. This is a key step because it alleviates lingering embarrassment.

3. Next, laugh it off! You can either laugh it off by yourself or with others. We recommend finding others who are

non-judgmental and supportive who you can laugh with. This helps normalize laughing at your setbacks and helps give you perspective.

4. View your setback as an opportunity. At least it's a great story to tell! At most, it's an opportunity to learn where you can improve.

5. Reflect. If your setback took place in a business setting, make sure to take note of it so you can avoid it in the future!

Lastly, and most importantly, stay curious. If you are reading this, you're doing a great job of that already!

Like Dweck, we can look to children to show us the way. Children's brains are more inclined to be curious. Because they don't have a cache of experiences to help inform them about their surroundings (and any potential dangers in said surroundings), their brain is a sponge, ready to

absorb everything. Adult brains, by contrast, already draw from a well of experience. So, when met with a new one, they will simply categorize it as whatever it most closely resembles. Life is more efficient that way, but it puts us at an incredible disadvantage.

Awareness of Growth Mindset

At its core, understanding the growth mindset liberates us by resetting our belief of what we are capable of. As we learn and grow throughout our lifetime, the growth mindset defines your intelligence as fluid, directly impacted by the effort applied in wanting to further develop your capacity to learn.

It means that through increased awareness of your response, and the adoption of simple and deliberate pivots in those responses, your ability to learn can be radically altered. It's not the latest feel-good fad, this is indeed mind-hacking. But not the bad type! You have absolute control here.

Take a deeper dive into the groundbreaking work done by Carol Dweck and her team of researchers and academics, who sent waves of excitement through the existing understanding of mental models upon publishing the 2012 book "Mindset".

While Dweck's work has been instrumental in developing early childhood education and communication, this HBR article helpfully unpacks the concepts for application by adults and organisations. Further simplifying the concept, James Clear has created a helpful graph on a blog exploring the layers of behaviour change. Critically, he sums up that long-lasting change comes from placing focus on fundamental behaviours, and not on results. This is how we acquire skills. This is how the growth mindset enables and empowers people to achieve incredible personal growth and mastery.

So how important is the growth mindset for people wanting to make positive change?

Critical!

Anybody wishing to innovate and bring new means of solving problems at scale must engage with a growth mindset. Just as nobody is born a brilliant musician, a sharp accountant, or a swift lawyer, nobody is born with the skills and behaviours that they need to navigate the changing world of social enterprise and innovation. The traits of successful leaders and changemakers we admire don't come easy. In fact, they are learned and hard-won. They are not gifted.

Asking for help

Bringing any idea to life, let alone one aiming to create positive social change in equal measure to financial return, will require learning. Quoted in the SBT_UK "Unlocking Growth" guide, the CEO of Shakespeare Schools Foundation, Ruth Brock, talks about asking for help within a team:

"It's the adage about having the confidence to recruit people who are better than you and that's when you'll do better. But having the confidence to say <<help>> to someone in your team can still be a really difficult thing to do."

This is where the growth mindset plays a critical role. We can all relate to the comment above, asking for help can equate to admitting defeat in our minds; it can be perceived, as a sign of failure. However, a growth mindset allows us to equate asking for help with a sign of strength.

Practising the Growth Mindset

In practice, the task of asking for help, as reframed by a growth mindset, involves embracing the following thought patterns:

"If I fail, it actually means that I'm no good."

Evolves to *"Failure will happen. So when it does, I will learn. Fast."*

"The outcomes I expect in life are determined by my abilities."

Evolves to – *"The outcomes I can expect in life are the direct result of my attitude and the effort I put in."*

"I'm either good at things, or I'm simply not – I don't have the talent."

Evolves to – *"With sufficient time and focus I can learn anything I want to."*

The power of this simple pivot in approach cannot be overstated. As the thought patterns above are applied, the possibilities of what can be achieved by one person become vast; and if there's a team involved, then they become limitless.

The challenges that you will face as you set about making a positive change in the world are going to range from minor irritation to seemingly insurmountable obstacles. The growth mindset is the cheapest, simplest, and most fundamental tool to empower you to realise your vision. Start by identifying the fixed-mindset thought patterns and pivoting them with the growth mindset perspective. You have complete control over responses once you get used to halting fixed thoughts and substituting them with those that enable growth. The results will quickly follow.

The Growth Mindset Will Revolutionize Your Life

If you have a growth mindset, it means you're perceiving things that happen to you in the belief that your talents aren't fixed, but fluid. You believe that through hard work, dedication, and asking for help from those around you, you can improve your intelligence and ability to learn new skills. You're not worried about what others might think when you experience a setback, as you see it as par for the course and a natural part of the learning process. You put your energy into learning and not into worrying.

On the other hand, if you have a fixed mindset, you believe that you were born with your gifts and talents and that there's nothing you can do to change them. You're either naturally smart, or you're not, and no amount of trying can change that. This mentality also means that you're less motivated to push yourself. Your priority is simply to avoid failure, and you know that learning something new will involve setbacks.

It's Not Just For Kids

Although the research was originally conducted on school-age children, it's been recognized that these mindsets follow us into adulthood and can impact our professional lives and even our personal lives. These mindsets aren't limited to the way we pick up knowledge, but can apply to our personality traits, too. If we're convinced that we were born a certain way, such as antisocial or timid, and that's that, then, well, that will be that. But if we embrace the idea that, with a little effort, we can grow, evolve and mold ourselves to become what we wish to be, then we can achieve change we never thought possible.

Education and learning don't stop the moment you leave school or university. Life is one long lesson, and if we're not open to accepting and even welcoming failure as a sign that we're moving forward, then we are sure to stagnate.

If you can train yourself to perceive the world with a mindset of growth and open possibility, you'll be amazed at the benefits that you'll unlock in your relationships, career, state of mind, and health.

The Benefits Of A Growth Mindset

1. ***You Can Nourish Your Relationships:*** Dr. Dweck pointed out that growth mindsets can make a huge difference in all types of relationships.

A person with a fixed mindset expects a romantic relationship to be perfect, and refuses to accept the idea that a successful relationship will require work. To them, any type of effort would mean that the connection is fatally flawed. If they believe we all come to this world fully formed and unable to learn and adapt, then, logically, they also believe a relationship that's less than perfect will always be so. They want to be placed firmly on a pedestal by their lover, and they see any disagreements as disastrous rather than natural and inevitable.

Someone with a growth mindset, however, understands that two people coming together will always have their differences. They get the fact that a relationship involves both parties learning about the other and growing together, developing the skills they need to work well as a team. This isn't just true of romantic relationships. Platonic and familial relationships also need work and nourishment, something which a fixed mindset struggles to comprehend.

2. ***You Judge Yourself And Others Less:*** If we have a fixed mindset, our reflex is always to judge and evaluate the things that are going on around us.

    Everything that happens is used to assess things, like whether or not we're a good person or whether we're doing better than the person at the next desk.

    A growth mindset doesn't have time to waste on proclaiming judgment or on what other people are doing; such an individual is too busy focusing on how he or she can bring about progress.

3. ***You Thrive Off Constructive Criticism:*** There are few more valuable skills than being able to accept constructive criticism and use it as a platform for growth.

If you can see criticism as an opportunity to improve rather than take it to heart, there will be no stopping you.

In the same way, a growth mindset means that you don't need constant validation to reassure you that you're getting things right.

4. You Chill Out And Enjoy The Ride: If you're always worrying about failure, you'll never have any fun.

As Dweck put it, "You don't have to think you're already great at something to want to do it and to enjoy doing it."

Since what you're focused on is the learning part, it doesn't matter whether or not you succeed; you can still have a great time giving it a shot. That means you can try out new sports or new hobbies without a shred of embarrassment over your lack of prowess, opening the door to all kinds of ways of enjoying yourself that you never even knew existed.

1. *You Tackle The Hardest Task On Your To-do List First:* Those of us with fixed mindsets excel at procrastination. They'll tick off all the easy things on their to-do list; those that they can do with our eyes closed. And they will put off doing anything that will actually require a modicum of thought or effort because they are worried that they won't rise to the challenge.

Someone with a growth mindset, on the other hand, relishes a challenge. They get stuck straight into the hardest task on their list, enjoying the chance to learn something new and improve their skills and knowledge. A growth mindset can do wonders for productivity.

2. **You Stop Stressing:** With a fixed mindset, the focus is constantly on success. You can't ever let your standards slip, and always have to be perfect because of what you believe a mistake would say about you.

    When you look at the world through the eyes of a fixed mindset, one bad test result defines you forever. If that's the way you approach things in life, stress is inevitable.

    Imagine how relaxed you'd feel if you just no longer cared. With a growth mindset, your only focus is on improving, with no element of worry about what anyone else thinks. In other words - Liberation.

3. **You Lower Your Risk Of Experiencing Depression:** Various studies have shown that looking at life through the lens of a fixed mindset can increase your risk of depression.

    It's logical, when you think about it, as you take any setbacks far more seriously. You can start to question your abilities and even who you are as a person.

    With a growth mindset, however, you no longer expect perfection, so you won't be as likely to experience anxiety and depression when you fail.

4. **You Gain More Perspective:** If you have a growth mindset, you can appreciate the fact that the break-up of a relationship or a bad exam result do not define who you are as a person or mean the world is about to end.

You know that your intelligence can't be summed up by a number and your self-worth doesn't depend on whether or not your relationship stands the test of time.

5. ***You're Not Afraid To Dream Big:*** If your fixed mindset is focused on your next test score or generally worrying about how you'll perform in individual events, it will never dare to dream.

   A fixed mindset is scared to set its sights too high because it only thinks about how awful the fall might be.

   By contrast, a growth mindset is able to focus on the end goal and doesn't let individual setbacks knock it off course.

Growth Mindset Powers Positivity

"Well, it's a high-risk project, but I thought if I don't try there's zero chance for this to happen."

Boyan Slat, reflecting on his decision to drop out of Aerospace Engineering studies at the University of Delft. Deciding to focus on ridding the oceans of plastic pollution.

Boyan Slat's The Ocean Cleanup project had humble beginnings. Founded in 2013, it consumed Slat's entire budget (three hundred Euros of pocket money he had saved) from the very first step, when the foundation registration fee had to be paid. Since Slat had written to hundreds of companies seeking sponsorship, the rejection seemed to be as large as the great Pacific garbage patch itself; Boyan acknowledges that he had little understanding of the task at hand. But passion and determination fueled him, as did an infectious positivity and a desire to learn (growth mindset!). These qualities kept him on the right path.

Today, The Ocean Cleanup has over 80 staff members and has raised over $30 million in funding, mostly from donations. Many will know this project as one of the most successful crowdfunding campaigns in history. Many of you will not know that the original technical designs were so flawed that the project nearly derailed.

Boyan Slat's journey and that of the project he founded has been marked by a series of failures followed by pivots. Failure followed by pivot. Failure followed by pivot; the mark of a growth mindset.

Changing Your Mindset Can Change Your Life

You can't figure it out. You haven't figured it out yet. Which of those describe you when you face a challenge?

If you believe you can't do something because you aren't smart enough or lack the skills to address the problem, you have a fixed mindset.

A fixed mindset focuses on the negative, is deficit-based, and keeps you stuck in the current situation. Your chance of getting a promotion or a raise is slim if you don't believe in yourself or your abilities to improve and grow.

If you haven't figured it out yet but you are working on the problem or seeking another solution to it, you have a growth mindset.

A growth mindset is positive, strength-based and focuses on the future. If you seek opportunities to learn, are ambitious, and use constructive criticism to refine your skills, you have a much better chance of being successful.

Hopefully, you can see why it's so important to learn about mindset and how it affects your behavior. As Dweck explains, it is more challenging than you think to make the shift – especially if you've had a fixed mindset for many years. But you'll probably agree that making the change to a growth mindset is more important than ever.

CHAPTER 6

THE IMPORTANCE OF CREATING A MINDSET FOR SUCCESS

Success is a choice, and choosing to be successful - in family life, in business, in relationships, in health - is a matter of deciding to set goals and attain them. Reaching goals does not have to be an overwhelming prospect, though. Creating a mindset that welcomes success is about taking small steps toward a larger objective.

"It is not always the people who start out the smartest who end up the smartest."

Alfred Binet.

Your success quotient is made up of skills, knowledge and attitude, with attitude accounting for 85%. Carol S. Dweck's book, "Mindset The New Psychology for Success", stresses how important attitude is, but also adds an additional premise according to which you have to be open to learning rather than closed and reluctant. According to Dweck, the world is divided between people who do and don't have an open mindset. Those who do have an open mindset succeed, often outperform and lead happier lives as compared to those with exceptional skills and knowledge but who have a closed mindset.

Strong differences in people's backgrounds, experiences, education and training have all been used as a way to explain why some of us achieve success and many of us fall short. According to Dweck, mindsets frame the running account taking place in people's heads. They guide how you interpret things. The fixed mindset tends to judge failure as a loss and re-enforces its view of failure with internal monologues such as: "This means I am a loser," or "This means I am not as good as they are." It also tends to support shutting down, not trying again or giving up. Growth mindset people, on the other hand, monitor negative situations and have internal dialogues with themselves, but they also interpret failure as a challenge and a learning experience. They know that they can obtain both positive and negative lessons from failure experiences. They tend to look at failure as constructive, as an opportunity for growth. They ask questions like: "What can I learn from this," or "How can I improve?"

Dweck suggests that there are four key steps to shifting your closed mindset to a more open one. It is also important to note that many of us have both mindsets and they come into play in different situations. So, when facing a future challenge, setback or criticism, you might decide that your fixed talents or abilities are lacking. Alternatively, you can try a growth mindset approach that suggests you need to ramp up your efforts, stretch yourself and possibly train and enhance your skills and abilities.

Here are some suggested steps:

1. *Learn to identify and hear your fixed mindset voice:* Look at situations and ask yourself about your judgments

and your response to the situation. Are you inclined to say things like: "It's not too late to back out, make excuses," or "It's not my fault?"

2. ***Recognize that you do have a choice:*** Interpreting situations as bad or as a setback can often be shifted to viewing them as a learning experience and a stepping stone to success. The choice is really up to you.

3. ***Talk back to yourself with a growth mindset voice:*** A fixed mindset voice can say things like: "Are you sure you can do this? Maybe you don't have the talent." On the other hand, a growth mindset voice might say: "I may not be able to do this right now, but I can learn it with time and help."

4. ***Take a growth mindset action step:*** Since everything is up to you, you can also control what you say and hear. Learn from your setbacks and try again. Take on challenges, and when you hear criticism, act on it. This is not always easy, but practice, with the support of a coach or mentor, can make all the difference in enhancing your success quotient score and getting attitudes in place for enhanced success.

How To Have The Mindset For Success

Learning how to have the mindset for success is crucial when you want a prosperous and blissful life. If you are like me, you might have many goals you want to achieve. Whatever these goals are, the key to actually fulfilling them is a growth mindset rather than a fixed one. But what is the difference and how can you get the results you need?

Open Mindset

How can you set out to adopt the mindset for success? Do you want to reach your goals more rapidly? In how many years are you planning to achieve your goals?

Many people, just like me, preach hard work, focus, persistence and more, but these are by-products of something else. It is something much more powerful than we can all develop. This extraordinary thing is critical to success - and it is your very own mindset.

Without the right mindset, you might find yourself sidetracked by your everyday routine. You can often be distracted by the latest and – at least in appearance – most fabulous idea that's just crossed your mind, which rarely pushes you to follow one path until actually reaching success.

You may think that you have all the time in the world to achieve your goals. But you have to realize that if you set your mindset for success, you can apply it to other domains as well. In this way, you will reach your goals much faster and find that you possess the capacity to form new and bigger goals.

The Trap of the Mindset

It is always better to fail many times before succeeding, as this will help you avoid many psychological traps. One of the most common traps is to believe that you are smarter than other people, that you do not have to work hard because you have talent, or that you have nothing left to learn.

You should know that the right mindset does not require you to possess extraordinary intelligence or be gifted with talents.

"The moment you believe that success is determined by an ingrained level of ability, you will brittle in the face of adversity." - Josh W., International Chess champion

So, as soon as you think success is determined by talent, you become weak in the face of obstacles.

The Difference between a Fixed and a Growth Mindset

So, as soon as people see intelligence or abilities as fixed, they believe that many things are impossible for them to achieve because they put limits on themselves and their skills. And that is what is called a fixed mindset.

But other persons see abilities as qualities that can be developed, which is, in this case, called a growth mindset. The important part is that those two different frames of mind lead to contrasting behaviors and results.

When you have a growth mindset, you know you can change your intelligence and increase your aptitudes and skills over time. By contrast, people with a fixed mindset do not think this is possible. So, the difference between the two groups is the perspective on intellect and brainpower.

The Possibility of a Different Mindset

Many studies have shown similar effects of the mindset on any ability, ranging from problem-solving all the way to playing sports or managing teams of people. The key to success is not merely effort, focus or resilience, but rather the growth mindset that creates the rest.

Your mindset is critical. When you try to improve your sense of determination or persistence directly, it is not nearly as effective as when addressing the mind-frame that underlies these traits. How many people think of themselves as not creative, not sociable, math-oriented, or even athletic? On the other hand, some people may think that they are naturals. If you tant to fulfill your full potential, you need to think differently. More specifically, you need to realize that you are not chained to a given set of current capabilities and that you can modify your mindset.

A Mindset Can Be Changed

You should know that your brain is very malleable, a feature known as plasticity. This means that you can change the way you think and perform. In fact, many of the accomplished people of our era were at least once in their lives told by so-called experts that they have no chance of a successful future. People like Charles Darwin, Marcel Proust, and many others.However, they, along with all the other high-achievers, continued to build and further develop their abilities.

The vital thing here is to realize that you can change your abilities and picture yourself where you want to be. When you have a growth mindset, you bring your game to new levels. So, how does a growth frame of mind do that?

Well, there are biological manifestations of the mindset. Tests shows that, in people who have a fixed mindset, the brain becomes most active when they receive information about how they perform. By contrast, people with a growth mindset have a particularly active mind when they receive information about what they could do better next time.

The Choice of a Growth Mindset

In other words, people with a fixed frame of mind worry most about being judged, while those with a growth mindset focus most on learning. There are other consequences of one's outlook, too. A fixed mind sees effort as a bad thing, something that only people with low capabilities need, while those with a growth approach see effort as something that makes them smart, in other words a way to grow.

When they hit a setback or failure, people with a fixed mindset tend to conclude that they are incapable, so in order to protect their ego, they lose interest or withdraw. This attitude is often taken as a lack of motivation, but behind it lies a fixed frame of mind.

On the other side of the spectrum, people with a growth frame of mind believe that setbacks are a part of personal development. They find a way around the problem.

So, what does all of this means for you? That you have to challenge yourself. It also means that you have to praise yourself for being great at something or for being smart. Do not forget to also honor others, especially children, for the same things.

Your Mindset Affects Everything

Trying hard pushes you to work even harder the next time you face a challenge. Do not get into the fixed-mindset way of thinking that when you win, you are a winner, and when you lose, this must make you a loser. The reason behind this type of attitude is that your mindset affects your performance.

Remember that you can change your mindset any time you wish. When you teach or have a growth mindset, not only it improves you as an all, but it also narrows down the achievement gap.

The mindset affects all of us. At the workplace, managers and supervisors with a fixed mindset do not accept much feedback and they do not mentor people. A wrong-or-right frame of mind even affects relationships, sports, and health.

Why do schools not teach the growth mindset to children instead of being so critical?

Tips to Have the Mindset for Success

- Get a growth mindset.
- Develop success habits.
- Understand that a growth mindset is beneficial.
- Know that your brain changes when you work hard to improve yourself.
- Make a small step toward each of your goals every day.

- Learn how to develop your abilities while also teaching others to do the same.
- Capture all of the information that could help you.
- Do a deliberate daily practice to develop your abilities through effective effort.
- Listen to audio books or learn a new language on your phone while you are out for a walk instead of listening to music.
- Clip articles and inspiring ideas for a vision board.
- Learn from your failures by asking yourself what you learned from the experience.
- Know your strengths and weaknesses.
- Develop core skills that will help you achieve your goals.
- After experiencing a setback, do not dwell on it. Instead, make an evaluation and move on to the next thing.

If you have the right mindset, tthis will allow you to succeed beyond all your expectations. You have to learn to talk back with a growth mindset voice when you listen and hear your fixed mindframe. Therefore, when you hear the inner voice saying "You can't," just add another word to this awful sentence – "Yet."

Cultivating a Success Mindset

According to a study published in the journal Psychological Science, evidence suggests that the individuals who believe that they can improve their level of intelligence are more likely to be successful in the long run.

In the study, subjects wore a special 'cap' that recorded their electrical brain activity while completing certain letter puzzles. These puzzles were specifically designed for participants to make mistakes. What researchers found was that when participants made mistakes, their brain sent two quick signals. The first was a quick recognition of the error (what Michigan State University psychology professor Jason Moser refers to as the 'oh crap response') and a second signal that indicated a willingness to get it right.

Those participants with a growth mindset, a belief that their hard work will pay off for them in the long run, had a much stronger second signal and were more likely and willing to correct their mistakes. They saw a net advantage in doing so. In essence, this group saw their errors as opportunities to grow, improve and learn, rather than an indication of their lack of capability.

It is this belief that you can continue to learn, grow and improve that serves to establish the Success Mindset. Successful people do not look to their failures as indications of what they can't do, but as learning opportunities instead. They recognise that their errors are merely indications of what they didn't know, but need to learn... and then they go out and learn it!

The Work:

Consider what your typical response is when you fail or find yourself faced with a setback What is your self-talk like immediately following such an event? Are you more likely to to use the event to validate the thoughts as to why you shouldn't have tried in the first place, or is your self-talk aimed at convincing you that you will succeed in the future with a little more direction, information or coaching?

If it's the former, we need to work at rewiring your belief systems, to shift your perspective to that Success Mindset. Instead of believing that your intellect is entirely pre-determined, recognise that you can develop and grow your intelligence through hard work. If you are willing to put in the work, you can minimize your errors in the future.

Mindset is Important for the Success of Every Entrepreneur

If you start your entrepreneurial journey with the mindset that you may fail, you are doomed. Having the right mindset is the foremost attribute of every entrepreneur. If there is something that the world's most successful entrepreneurs - Microsoft's Bill Gates, Wal-Mart's Sam Walton, IBM's Thomas Watson Sr, or GE's Thomas Alwa Edison – have in common, it is their winning mindsets. A great product or idea will not necessarily ensure success in business. It is with positive mindsets that these industry leaders built thriving companies.

Open Mindset

Even if your entrepreneurial venture is small, with very limited operations, the most vital element for its success is your mindset. It's always a roller coaster ride for an entrepreneur. Every entrepreneur must be confident about handling the everyday pressures and setbacks that are bound to happen in any business. The way you react to such situations largely depends on your mindset. However bleak the scenario may be, you can take control of it with your confidence. An optimistic mindset will help you accept failures and learn from them.

Keeping a positive mindset is of prime importance for you to focus on your entrepreneurial goals and work hard toward achieving them. Nevertheless, being a workaholic is not an appreciable trait, as it will burn you out sooner or later. What counts is your ability to put in long hours when required, and this will only come with a mindset tuned for success.

As an entrepreneur, you are free to do what you want, but a successful entrepreneur is well disciplined and responsible. It is critical to have a mindset that welcomes accountability along with freedom. A good entrepreneur enjoys the freedom to explore and choose the line of business, set goals and strategies, and make crucial decisions. At the same time, he or she accepts the accountability to customers, employers, and other stakeholders. With this mindset alone, any business can be run professionally with the aim of being successful in the long run.

It is important to keep your ego at bay when you venture out to be an entrepreneur. Rejections and rebukes can occur during the course of running any enterprise. With an open and ego-less mindset, you will be able to accept them and move on. An entrepreneur with a winning attitude will not allow such situations to hamper his or her pursuit of success.

While having a single-minded quest for success is necessary, an entrepreneur needs to have a flexible mindset that can easily adapt to changes. Things may not always turn out as you had planned. When new opportunities emerge, an open mind is required to change your pre-decided course of action and take new routes. An adaptable mindset also helps you learn and grow.

Finally, for an entrepreneur, an altruistic mindset is not an always appreciable trait when it comes to making money from business. A good entrepreneur must not shy away from making money. The way you want to spend the money made is up to you, but wealth creation must be one of your primary goals as an entrepreneur. A mindset that values wealth will lead you to become a successful entrepreneur.

5 Important Steps to Develop a Mindset For Success and Become a Client-Attraction Magnet

Your mindset is the key to your success. How you view something will determine your response. Something as intangible as your thoughts and feelings determine your actions. The good news is that you have a choice and change can happen. In fact, it does not even need to be a long drawn out

Open Mindset

painful process. Before anything changes, you need to make the choice to take action. Embrace the willingness to examine your beliefs. Determine which are working for you and which are ready for a tune-up.

Ready to get started? Here are 5 steps to begin developing a mindset for success and becoming a client-attraction magnet.

1. **Desire to make a change:** Having a desire to do things differently is significant. A willingness to explore all options is the first step toward creating a mindset for success. Be ready to step out of the box. Be adventurous by opening your mind to alternative perceptions. Explore the infinite possibilities of perceptions. Instead of focusing on negative perceptions, begin to develop beliefs which are positive and build you up.

2. **Who you spend time with:** *"You are the average of the five people you spend the most time with."* (Jim Rohn) The people you surround yourself with will affect your mindset. Think about them. If you are spending time with people who are also forward-thinkers and understand your excitement and drive, you are in good company. On the other hand, if you are surrounded by people who always seem to go from one crisis to another and you appear to be the solution to their problems, your energy will be drained.

One of the most difficult things to do, but also necessary for moving forward, is to look at the people in your life. Are they driven to live their life with purpose and understand your desire for success?

Choose people who will build you up. Connect with people who are already achieving some of the goals you are currently striving for. Remember, if you want to be a millionaire, you need to spend time with millionaires. They think differently and act differently than people living paycheck to paycheck.

3. ***Know what holds you back:*** Everything you do is based upon your beliefs. In turn, this affects how you perceive the world around you. Put your finger on what is holding you back and getting in the way of your success. If you don't have any negative beliefs about success, then analyze your beliefs concerning money and wealth. They are related, but different.

Look within and decide if there is a difference between what you say you want and what you actually believe is true. Your core beliefs were influenced by your life circumstances and how you interpreted those events. Look back on those events or influences. How old were you?

Unless you have consciously done your work, you will be surprised to find out that beliefs you developed at a much younger age continue to influence your mindset. This is like having a young child get into the driver's seat of the bus and begin driving the bus. If the old belief does not work for you, blow it up! That is right. Let it go. Create one that is more relevant to who you are now and your current life goals.

4. ***Action vs. Avoidance:*** Changing your beliefs and how you view your circumstances is crucial. When you are ready, take action. Understand that the last part of the word "attraction" is action.

Open Mindset

If avoidance has kept you in a comfortable place and contributed to your current situation, then you need to do something different to break out of your comfort zone. Your comfort zone is familiar and predictable.

Continuing with the status quo helps to avoid disappointment and pain. It is almost a catch-22 situation. You are dissatisfied with your current level of success, but the pain and dissatisfaction are not great enough for you to break your own glass ceiling.

In order to create a successful business, you need to "show up" differently. Having the mindset for success motivates you to take action and step out of your comfort zone. You will be driven to do things you never would have considered as options. In fact, settling for mediocrity will not be an option anymore. How cool is that?

Make the choice to stretch yourself beyond what you thought was possible. By making this mindset shift and beginning to take action, you will implicitly step toward your life's purpose.

Feel the energy shift. Your vibration will rise and people will notice. What you have to do in order to succeed might not change. The way you approach taking those steps will change significantly. Having confidence and taking action with a mindset for success is very attractive to clients.

5. ***Identify your purpose:*** Deep down connect with the very thing that drives you. Find out what your gift is, your special talent. Get really clear about it. Discard the excuses for not taking action and following through with your

passion. They have only kept you from taking bold steps towards success.

Now that you are feeling your vibration rise, that feeling of excitement as you make a correction, you will embrace a "do anything" mindset. Watch opportunities appear. This will only happen if you make the conscious decision of embracing your purpose.

Set an intention for yourself and envision yourself as a successful person. Get out of your head and wonder how you are going to do it. Connect with your heart, knowing you have all the answers within you. You have a gift to share; an obligation to be of service and to help others.

Create boundaries and surround yourself with like-minded people. Surround yourself with people who understand your passion and share similar goals. Don't wait for them to find you, take the initiative and seek them out.

Reframe your core beliefs. Instead of focusing on limitations and what is not going well, putting out one crisis after another, focus on moving toward your vision and your goal. Focus on your capabilities and feel like a success, acting "as if".

Taking action is very attractive to clients. The Law of Attraction loves quick, decisive action. Stay in the moment, believe in yourself and embrace a feeling of confidence in the gifts you have to offer.

Become a client-attraction magnet by changing focus, changing how you respond, taking action on opportunities which appear out of the blue, and feeling confident.

Empower yourself and watch the domino effect unfold before your eyes. As you discard a negative belief for a positive intention, there will be a domino effect leading you to success. The amazing part is that all you need to do is make the choice to embrace a mindset for success and the rest will follow.

CHAPTER 7

THE IMPORTANCE OF COMMITMENT TO ACHIEVING SUCCESS

The majority of people fear success. Fear of the unknown, poor self-esteem and fear of failure are factors that prevent us from setting and, more importantly, achieving our goals. Fear is largely the result of the conditioning process. Sometimes, in trying to protect their children from disappointments in life, parents stop yearning or aiming for more, and this attitude of "be happy with what you have" is permanently enforced upon youngsters. This is all about mindset.

The pattern is then set for life; a pattern of:

1. No goals in life, as they do not understand the importance thereof.

2. Fear of taking on any challenging tasks.

3. Feeling beaten before attempting.

4. Being influenced by third parties to such an extent that they have no control over their lives.

5. Low self-esteem, blaming luck or fate for their failures.

Open Mindset

How do you change this fear to your own benefit?

Fear can have a very positive side-effect if you know how to apply it. Everybody makes mistakes, but you need to avoid making the same mistake twice. You need to use this fear and failure as tools to help you learn and grow in experience and knowledge. Learn to profit from an environment where you can commit errors and develop yourself. The best remedy for fear is taking action.

Remember, "when the going gets tough, the tough gets going". Get the right mindset by visualizing the mistakes you have made in the past, then move to a next super-level of visualization where you are in total control because you can see yourself achieving success and avoiding previous mistakes. Focus on this daily, and you can reprogram your subconscious to expect success.

Success is to decide exactly what you want, bearing in mind the benefits and disadvantages, achieving a balance between what you want and the sacrifices you will have to make, and then achieving it. If you were suppressed by your parents, you need to know there is another life out there! You need to set goals for yourself and decide how to achieve them. Even if achieving your life goals means deviating from your planned actions, everything is worth it as long as you get there stronger and better. Knowing your goals, identifying what you need to achieve them and setting a timeframe in which to complete them will put you on the road of success. To get results, emulate role models. A healthy body and mind are two things everyone should aim for.

Life-Changing Decisions You Must Make To Achieve Success

Dr. Wayne Dyer said, "It is not what is in this world that determines the quality of your life, it is how you choose to process your world in your thoughts." Similarly, Norman Vincent Peale said, "Change your thoughts and you change your world." A number of other experts have also stressed the importance of changing our thoughts or mindsets in order to achieve success in life. Even though a person's success depends upon innumerable factors, which include traits such as commitment, determination and a willingness or readiness to sacrifice, none of these is as important as possessing the right mindset. Let us delve deeper into this:

1. ***Realize that every stumbling block comes with an opportunity:*** During the course of your journey towards success, you may face several hurdles. Instead of viewing them as failures, you must find out the kernel of opportunity those hurdles provide. For example, if you have not landed a job despite putting forth the required efforts, you can view this as an opportunity to start your own business. Another alternative is to think that this shows that you have to reinforce your efforts and learn more thoroughly in order to aim for a higher position. There is no doubt that such hurdles test how strong your determination and mental fortitude are. But if you continue your journey with added determination, you will taste success soon.

2. ***Complaining will take you nowhere:*** Failures, hurdles and difficulties may cause frustration, but if you

squander your time lamenting over them, you will not move an inch forward. Instead, you should probe into the reasons that have caused those hurdles and avoid repeating those mistakes. Such a mindset will fast-track your success.

3. ***Be ready for discomforts:*** Very often, you may have to get out of your comfort zone and push yourself. This may cause discomforts. You must be ready to subject yourself to such uncomfortable situations if you want to achieve success.

4. ***Be ready to take risks as often as possible:*** You must always be curious and learn new things. Such an attitude will help you find new opportunities that you have not known about earlier. If you take calculated risks, you can translate those opportunities into successful endeavors. By contrast, if you cozily remain within your comfort zone and never take risks, you will not be able to shape a great future for yourself.

5. ***Have self-belief:*** The most important mindset change you must make is to develop self- belief. If you believe in yourself, it will open new vistas that you have never explored before. In fact, believing in yourself helps you overcome your obstacles easily. This mindset change will hasten your success as well.

Developing a Success-Driven Mindset

Our personal growth is something that we should all strive for and it is what drives us forward in life. Anything else means you are standing still or going backwards. No one should ever want that for themselves and especially for their families. Nothing good is going to come to you if you stagnate, and even if it does, it does not last for long. There are times when you get that lucky break and the law of averages balances everything out, but all in all, it takes drive, desire, commitment and of course a little bit of work to bring a consistent level of growth and success to your life.

Developing a success-driven mindset is not something that comes to the majority of people who yearn for a better and more productive life, yet it is the very building block of success. Anyone who has ever achieved anything worthwhile in life knew in their own mind what it would take to get there, and more importantly, how to get there. They knew the secret of developing a success-driven mindset and the power that comes with it. This power is open to anyone who chooses to use it, but unfortunately for most, it is disregarded and never used to even a fraction of its potential.

While the visionaries and achievers of years gone by had to work it all out by themselves, nowadays the resources to become successful are all close to hand. The advent of the internet had a lot to do with it, but there were also books picking dust up on library shelves even if they contained the answers to questions that for years had been left unanswered. They still are for most people and will remain so, until all individuals make the decision to begin developing a success-driven mindset. Without the internet, these great classics would have probably remained unearthed, except for the very few.

In most cases, you do not even have to pay for the privilege of gaining this incredible knowledge. Do a simple search on the world wide web and you will find that the idea of developing a success-driven mindset is just a click away. Begin by reading a chapter a day of Napoleon Hills' "Think And Grow Rich", put the knowledge into action, and you will soon start developing a success-driven mindset. There is plenty of additional information available, from the old classics to the more modern interpretations.

The 7 Deadly Enemies of Goal-Achievement Success

"If there is no enemy within, then there's no enemy without."

If that sounds a little too cryptic, a little too metaphysical or a little too 'flaky', then let me explain it this way; the only true 'enemies' or obstacles to the achievement of your goals are the enemies and obstacles you yourself create within your own mind.

You see, greatness, that over-riding, all-consuming desire to be, do and have the extraordinary in your life is a choice that WE get to make rather than some external decision or some kind of 'luck' that only few of us will ever experience. Greatness is the combined effect of the various choices we make day in day out, week in week out, month in month out and year in year out, choices that shape our actions and, eventually, our destinies. Make great choices and your destiny (your destination in life) will be a great one; hence 'greatness'.

But if that is true (and it is), why is it that so many of us fail to make those great choices that could lead us to the achievement of the great life we all claim to crave and desire so much? Well, just a little examination reveals EXACTLY why we get pulled off course. There are 7 reasons. Let's take a look at them.

1. ***Indifference:*** It's crazy I know, but many people are just plain indifferent to creating a life of greatness. Sure, they may talk about what they'd like to do, they may say "Wouldn't it be nice if...", but for these people there's just never enough of a reason to actually get up and walk their talk.

That's a shame, really, because if they can think about having more, then they also have the ability to have more. All they're lacking in is a little passion, a reason, a WHY?

Having a powerful enough "why" would propel them into action faster than ever. In its absence, though, they simply talk and think about their dreams, without ever acting on any of them.

2. ***Indecision:*** Some people just can't make a decision. In fact, MOST people don't really know what a decision really is and so it's no wonder that they're stuck in that no man's land where they take no action whatsoever.

For the record, the word "decision" shares its Latin roots with the word "incision", and means "to cut off from all other possibility". Maybe that's why most people struggle with making decisions. They never truly cut themselves off from other options and so they to and fro, to and fro between actions, going pretty much nowhere... fast!

A decision about giving up on smoking means that you're not going to "try" to stop, but rather "That's it, I'm a non-smoker, I don't do that anymore"; a decision about losing 50lbs means that you're not going to drop your exercise plan or diet because it's going more slowly than you'd hoped, but rather "Ok, that just means it's going to take a little longer before I can eat my first ice-cream or eat my first chocolate bar, but I WILL NOT do so until I've hit my goal."

A decision adds amazing strength to any goal. Indecision weakens anything and everything about it.

If you haven't really made a decision, you haven't really set a goal.

3. *Doubt:* It's amazing how many people set out to pursue goals that they "know" in advance they cannot achieve.

Of course, there's no evidence that the goals are impossible, rather it's the individual's own mindset that says so; yet people still claim to be chasing the goals and say that they are important. Of course they're not! How can they be important and how can they possibly chase a goal that they "know" they can't ever get? It's all a show. Smoke and mirrors stuff that makes them look like they're being positive and proactive whilst actually looking at all the ways that they CAN'T have what they want.

Let me ask you, how hard would YOU work toward achieving something that you truly believed you could never have?

The answer is, you wouldn't. You'd take the minimum amount of action you could, then you'd tell everyone that the goal was unrealistic and wasn't meant to be, right?

What a shame! You don't even have to 100% believe you're going to have something come true for you. Sure, it's even better when you do, but for some of us that's a lot to ask, right? Instead, you can just agree to suspend disbelief.

That's it.

Just stop telling yourself why you can't have it. That's enough... for now.

4. ***Worry:*** You can't really separate worry from doubt. They're both sides of the same coin. When you doubt the outcome of something, you worry about what will happen instead. Will you waste time? Will you waste money? Will you look stupid? Will it cost you your job, your house, your relationship?

Worry can eat all of your personal power away to the point where it's easier to be indifferent and indecisive than it is to actually pursue the goals that would change your life for the better. Worry makes you freeze on the spot, wondering "What if it goes wrong?" instead of focusing on what it'll be like when you achieve your goals. Do you know what the simple cure for worries is, though? Simply focus on the other "what if". The "What if all this goes RIGHT?"

5. ***Excessive caution:*** Excessive caution is born out of worry. It's the same thing, only sneakier.

Excessive caution may allow you to take some actions toward your goals, but it'll always have you taking the teeniest-tiniest, tippy-toe steps toward them on the pretence of 'playing it safe' or 'reducing risk' rather than launching a full-scale 'assault' of your goals with all your motivation, all your inspiration, all your passion and all your purpose.

Do that and your goal achievement is certain, but excessive caution tells you that now is not the right time, it's best to be careful, to take it slow.

Excessive caution reminds you of the Lao-Tsu quote: "A journey of a thousand miles begins with a single step". However, it also happens to neglect the idea that the same 1000-mile journey can only be completed by continuing to take steps one after the other until the journey is complete.

6. **Pessimism:** This is the 'grown-up' hybrid of doubt, worry and excessive caution all rolled into one. But pessimism's more dangerous.

Pessimism doesn't hint at why something may not be possible, like doubt does; it doesn't make you take small half-hearted steps toward your goal, like worry does; and it doesn't have you advancing timidly, scared of what's around the corner, excessive caution does.

In fact, pessimism tells you straight out that what you want isn't possible, that it's not worth pursuing and that if you do it, then something is absolutely certain to go wrong.

Pessimism says to you "The mountain is too high, the path is too steep, the load too heavy and the reward too small, so why bother?" The good news is that pessimism can be killed off by its alter-ego... optimism.

Optimism is merely the sum total of expectation plus excitement. If you can get excited about something and truly work on expecting it to happen, then pessimism withers up, dies and bothers you no more.

7. **Complaining:** This is perhaps the most dangerous of all the enemies of goal achievement, as it combines all the other six and brings them into the world in a very real way.

When you give voice to your indifference, indecision, doubt, worry, excessive caution and pessimism, you start to verbally persuade both yourself and others about how unfair life is, how tough it is to get what you want, how hard you've tried yet how many times you've been let down and more.

When you do this, you create your own little pity-party, attracting others who agree with and reinforce your belief that you'll never get what you want from life and how deluded those 'positive thinking, goal setting weirdos' are.

Complaining is dangerous because it manifests negative thoughts into negative reality. At its worst, the 'dark side' of thoughts becomes actual reality.

Misery loves company. Don't give it any and it'll soon look elsewhere.

So there you have them, the 7 deadly enemies of goal achievement. Let them into your life and you're guaranteed a struggle with every single goal you set for yourself both now and in the future. On the other hand, if you learn to spot them and kick them out of your life right away, your achieving your goal is guaranteed.

Achieving Success With Positive Affirmations

Affirmations are statements that you think or say to yourself or others based on your beliefs. These affirmations can be either positive or negative, and can greatly influence your life and design your reality. As Brian Tracy said, "You become what you think about most of the time." In fact, affirmation is something that you do all the time. Every thought you think and every word you say is an affirmation. All of your inner dialogues are affirmations. You are continually affirming subconsciously, with your words and thoughts, and this flow of affirmations is creating your life experience in every moment.

You can achieve the success you desire by programming your mind with positive affirmations. In fact, most of the successful people in the world are not that different from you. The main difference between a successful person and an unsuccessful one is that most successful people have a success mindset. Their inner dialogue is one of success and accomplishment, and they always focus on the positive rather than on the negative.

Positive affirmations will be very useful to help you achieve the success you desire, and through the regular use of this powerful technique, you will begin to see wonderful changes in your life, changes you never imagined possible. With positive affirmations, you can overcome your limiting beliefs and negative thoughts, turning success into a reality for you. Ralph Marston once said, "There is a thought in your mind right now. The longer you hold on to it, the more you dwell upon it, the more life you give to that thought. Give it enough life, and it will become real. So make sure the thought is indeed a great one."

In order to achieve success, it is very important for you to develop a conscious and focused affirmation process. You must become aware of exactly what you are affirming through your thoughts, and consciously and purposefully focus those affirmations on positive and empowering statements. These positive affirmations will reprogram your subconscious mind and allow you to become more and more successful. By developing the habit of using positive affirmations regularly and consistently, your subconscious will adapt to the new information it is being provided with. For your affirmations to be effective, it is important that you create your very own, based on your specific conditions and circumstances. It is very important to remember that your affirmations are only going to be efficient if you can feel what you are affirming. It is the emotions that your affirmations create that will attract the success that you desire. The most effective positive affirmations are phrases that are in alignment with your beliefs, empower you and allow you to feel a shift in your emotions as you repeat them.

In order to become more successful, you can repeat the following affirmations or you can create your own ones:

1. I deserve to be prosperous and successful.

2. I enjoy success.

3. I am very successful now.

4. I am happy, successful, and fulfilled.

5. Success and achievement are natural outcomes for me.

6. I attract success and prosperity with all of my ideas.

7. Success comes very easily and effortlessly to me.

8. Today I am committed to my goals and my success is assured.

9. Everything I do turns into success.

10. My success is contagious, other people like it, seek it and respect it.

11. All of my thoughts and ideas lead me straight to success.

12. Prosperity and success are my natural state of mind.

13. I am a success magnet.

14. I am the example of success and triumph.

15. I am committed to achieving success.

You can all become as successful as you want by using positive affirmations regularly and consistently. Remember that success is a state of mind, and if you want success, you need to start thinking of yourself as a successful person. Henry David Thoreau was right when he said "As a single footstep will not make a path on the earth, so a single thought will not make a pathway in the mind. To make a deep physical path, we walk again and again. To make a deep mental path, we must think over and over the kind of thoughts we wish to dominate our lives."

Achieve Success by "Chunking it Down"

When we are faced with an enormous goal, project or task that we must complete, we are often so overwhelmed that we put off that project for another day. Then the next day comes and we are again faced with the challenging task, so what do we do? That's right – we decide to put it off another day. Our fear of tackling particularly large goals is often what causes the very procrastination that prevents us from completing the tasks at hand and implicitly achieving success. So what is the mindset necessary to overcome such obstacles? The simple mindset that you need to overcome huge challenges and reach complex goals is to simply cut those goals down into bite-sized chunks that you can eat one by one.

You Can't Swallow an Entire Steak

Imagine a nice juicy steak in front of you that you want to eat. If you don't like steak, well, just

work with me here. Now, swallowing that entire steak as a whole is simply impossible, no matter how hungry you are. Therefore, to accomplish the goal of devouring that steak, we do not try to shove the whole steak into our mouths. Instead, we pick up a knife and start slicing the meat into small bite-sized pieces that we can eat one bite at a time. The same holds true when it comes to fulfilling goals and dreams.

Slice Your Goals into Bite-Sized Pieces

The same concept of cutting the steak into bite size pieces and eating one piece at a time can be applied to all the large goals and challenges that you face in life. When presented with a large goal that seems overwhelming and impossible to conquer, our subconscious mind tells us that the task too big for us to handle. We never get round to working for that goal or project because it's psychologically intimidating. And let me tell you that life goals, projects and tasks are rarely accomplished in one single blow. In order to reach your goals, you must chop them up into bite-size pieces that you can eat one at a time. By doing it, the effort will no longer appear futile. It's important that you focus on eating that one bite-sized piece only, making sure that you chew fully, swallow it and then move onto the next piece. Here are some thoughts to remember:

- A little boy might look at the strongest, thickest tree in the forest and ask himself, "How can I ever fell this tree?" If the same boy took only a few chops of that tree with his axe a day, then no matter how mighty that tree is – it would eventually have to fall.

- Commit to doing five small things a day that move you in the direction of your goal. Small things add up to big things in the end, and if you just keep leaning into your goal, you will eventually succeed.

- Just like a human being can be broken down into a bunch of organs, cells, molecules, and elements, so can a goal be broken down into small pieces. Large goals are made up of smaller goals, and those smaller goals can be broken up into daily tasks. Break up your goals into as many small pieces as you can and complete a few of those tasks each day.

CHAPTER 8

HABITS OF SUCCESSFUL PEOPLE

Though everyone's definition of success is different, it is fairly easy to place the "successful" label on the person with the broad grin on their face, the one who seems to have it all figured out. Regardless of what you hope to become successful with, there are ways to move towards your goals and, eventually, conquer them.

The one thing I can guarantee that you will find with all of the world's most successful people is positive and healthy habits. Your habits are what define you as a person and the results you get in life. You can always look at someone's habits and tell if they are going to become successful or not, because success is as simple as the habits you have. Now that we understand the power of habits, it is time to look at how some of the most successful people in the world use habits to their advantage. You can use these people as your role models and create your own positive and healthy habits. Let's get into what these successful people do so differently by comparison with others.

First of all, successful people understand that even though motivating yourself and changing your state can be effective ways of working towards success, the foundation of all success is to control your habits at all times. These people use habits the same way a highly optimized factory would create their assembly line. The habits are constantly improved and adjusted, so that they perfectly fit the individual's needs and goals, but they also keep their fundamental structure of constant action untouched.

Today's most successful people come from all walks of life, but there are certain things virtually all of them have in common. Their success is the result of a mindset they share, which pushes them to seek out maximum efficiency. From the time they jump out of bed (usually very early), they begin employing habits that enable them to get more done by lunch than most people do all day. Their high productivity sets them apart from everyone else.

If you want to be successful, you must start by adopting the habits of successful people. This is because success is a journey, not a destination. Thus, it is what you do that will determine the results you get. In other words, it is your habits that will determine what you do, and what you do each day will determine what results you have in your life.

This is why success starts with adopting the habits that will bring you toward your goals and dreams. It is a known fact that it takes at least 30 days to create a new habit. Just imagine how life would be knowing that, after we change something for the better, that something brings success into our lives. 30 days is a very short period of time in the big scheme of things. So why is it so difficult to embrace the change that will enhance our lives? Successful people have bad habits, too. The main difference is that they know what

Open Mindset

these bad habits are and consciously work to counteract them.

In my view, successful people have a daily routine that unfolds in pretty much the same way every day, even if what actually takes place during the day may appearvery different. Successful people have defined the daily patterns that work best for them. Remember, if there was a recipe for success, we would have all bought the book! These daily habits are and will continue to be used by successful people.

1. *Exercise:* There are many benefits of regular exercise, both to your physical and mental health. Successful people know it's also the best way to start your day, providing an energy boost that can carry you for several hours. The early sense of accomplishment you'll feel afterward can also get your day off to a better start, since you will have already knocked out one important task before breakfast. Even 15 minutes of exercise as soon as you get out of bed can help restore your sense of alertness.

2. *Eat breakfast:* It's been said that breakfast is the most important meal of the day, and if you're looking to become successful, this is something you should incorporate into your morning routine. Avoid eating anything that will leave you feeling full and lethargic. Instead, eat something small and healthy, such as an egg and some fruit. The egg will provide you with the much-needed protein, and a small amount of fruit will help keep your blood sugar steady, without risking a sugar crash.

3. ***Turn off your phone:*** Those fancy smartphones we rely on so heavily these days can become a crippling distraction for anyone who's trying to stay productive. Successful people know they have to discipline themselves and only use their cellphones to make calls, send text messages or use apps that are actually necessary or helpful. Keep the ringer off to avoid the temptation to check it whenever it makes a sound. After awhile, you'll probably forget your smartphone is even there.

4. ***Read the news only once:*** There's nothing wrong with reading the news in the morning to catch up with current events. However, it can become a problem when you're checking it constantly throughout the day. In fact, the same can be said of social media sites, too. Going over them once in the morning is enough. Successful people know that at some point, you have to put these distractions aside and take care of the day's business.

5. ***Avoid negative people:*** If you haven't already noticed, negative people are far less likely to achieve high levels of success. According to renowned businessman Jim Rohn, each of us is an average of the five people we spend the most time with. What that implies is that if you want to become successful, you should be spending your time with positive and successful people. Procrastinators, complainers and perpetually angry individuals have a way of bringing others down. Avoid them whenever possible.

6. **Reward yourself:** One of the best ways to stay motivated is to continually reward yourself for achieving your objectives. If your idea of a treat is a triple espresso at your

favorite coffee shop, make that your reward for those extra tasks you knocked out before lunch. Just make sure you actually take some time during the day to enjoy these rewards.

7. ***Have an End in Mind:*** Before you can accomplish a goal, you need to figure out what that goal is. By clearly defining a goal to yourself, you put yourself into a "no compromises" position. Internal pressure and the excitement of the end result motivate you to move forward with your project, rather than stop halfway through.

That being said, it is a good idea to ensure that the goal is attainable. If you are aiming high, try breaking the goal down into smaller, bite-sized chunks. This helps you feel you are moving forward with the project, rather than get the impression that you will never finish the job.

8. ***Have a Schedule:*** Many people feel that there are not enough hours in a day to allow them to finish all the tasks they need to take care of. The best way around this issue is to be selective about how you spend your time. If you have work that needs to be done, set aside a certain amount of time for you to work on it. This helps you to avoid the pitfalls of excuses like "I will finish it after this", which evolves into "I do not have time today. Maybe I will do it tomorrow".

The downfall of this is quite obvious. Procrastination stems from a lack of structure, and structure requires a schedule. Even a loose idea of when you can work on something is far better than no idea at all.

9. **Be Persistent:** Small failures are inevitable in any endeavour. By taking failures positively, rather than negatively, you have a higher chance of attaining success.

When you do fail, do not ignore it and push that aspect of whatever you are working on to the back burner. Attacking adversity head-on is the only way to overcome it, and this is best accomplished by simply trying again.

10. **Be Positive:** Negativity has rarely impacted a project positively. By finding the silver lining to any problems that may arise and approaching them with positivity, you will find it far easier to combat them. Additionally, looking at your endeavour in a positive light in general will help you accomplish what you desire. Knowing the good that could result from what you are working on can help you feel more motivated.

11. ***Communicate and Have a Team:*** Everyone needs help or a positive boost at some point, and having a team of cheerleaders, well-wishers, or helpers can provide this. Communicating effectively to each team member ensures different aspects will be taken care of as you planned, reducing mistakes and failure rates. A small group of people you can lean on and bounce ideas off of can lend creativity and stability to your work.

Contrary to popular belief, there's really nothing mysterious about achieving success. Ultimately, successful people get where they are through hard work, persistence, and adherence to good habits. If you can discipline yourself to make these basic habits part of your daily routine, you'll find that the hard work and persistence will come easier.

Open Mindset

Copy Successful People

Success has a different meaning for each individual on planet Earth. For some, it might be to have an abundance of money, for some, it might be to drive the car of their dreams, and for some, it might be to spend time with their families. Whatever it is that you perceive as success, there is a proven way to reach it. Find people that you view as successful. Do as they do, have the willingness to work hard, b patient, and chances are that you will be successful.

Most successful people are willing and able to help. There are a few basic steps anyone can follow to learn how to be successful.

1. What is success to you? Write it down and define your goal.

2. Know that there are going to obstacles, write them down and be ready for them when they arise.

3. Pinpoint what is keeping you from your goals. Get rid of that and apply new habits like successful people do.

4. Establish what actions will take you closer to your goal, write them down. Create a daily to-do list and complete those actions one by one. Write down 5 things that you can do today that will bring you closer to success. Do them every day for twelve months. If you stick to this plan, you will end up taking 4380 steps towards your goal every year.

5. Set timelines and deadlines. This will ensure that you don't procrastinate.

6. Stick to your plan, don't give up until you have reached your goal.

7. Be consistent. Stick it out for at least 12 months before you even think of giving up. Perseverance is the key. Successful people never give up.

Now, go look for a mentor and follow the simple steps. Remember, success does not come easily, but those who are willing to work for it will attain it.

CHAPTER 9

CHANGE THE WORLD THROUGH AN OPEN MINDSET FOR GOOD THINGS TO HAPPEN

You're up for a job you really want. You give your absolute best effort during the interview but don't get it. You feel like a failure. No, in fact you think you are a failure.

But what if you reflected on the experience instead of sinking into self-doubt? What would you do differently next time? Where do you know you performed well? You come to terms with the idea that not getting hired doesn't make you a failure — after all, you made it to the final round of interviews. Buoyed by these insights, you find yourself confidently preparing for your next interview, armed with what you learned this time around.

The only real difference between these two scenarios is mindset.

Mindset influences everything: self-esteem, health, relationships, and careers. Your mindset is often just as powerful as circumstances in determining the course of your life. Unlike random situations, however, mindset is something you can learn to control.

The three theories that follow can help radically reprogram your reactions to common experiences. While they may seem counterintuitive (Don't try to overhaul your life? Embrace failure? Love a stranger?), these tweaks to your usual ways of thinking can help you become wiser, more competent, and more fulfilled.

What's more, shifting your perspective is not all that difficult. And it can improve your life in profound ways, starting now.

Climb Mountains One Step at a Time

Consider the New Year's resolution. You've probably never resolved to wake up five minutes earlier each day, because that would not seem to require much ambition. A real resolution, many of us believe, means becoming a lark who gets up at 5 a.m., even if you've always been a night owl. It means quitting all sugar, including fruit, instead of simply cutting out soda. We often think there's no point in change unless we're going to change big.

But aiming for radical change practically guarantees our efforts will fall flat.

> *"Change doesn't happen until people alter their behavior, and they don't alter their behavior unless they start with the small,"* explains Harvard philosophy professor Michael Puett, Ph.D., in his book "The Path: What

Chinese Philosophers Can Teach Us About the Good Life", which he co-wrote with journalist Christine Gross-Loh.

Puett's students often tell him they've changed their lives as a result of taking his course, which explores key principles of the Chinese philosophers Confucius, Mencius, and others. But instead of focusing on abstract philosophical queries, like "What is the meaning of life?" or "Do we have free will?", the class ponders questions like this one, from Confucius: "How are you living your life on a daily basis?"

His students' "changed lives" are less dramatic, but more sustainable than you might think, says Puett. "Their changes are not of the <<big>> sort, like suddenly deciding to run off and do something radically different," he affirms. "Something like that would probably not actually affect how they live their everyday lives. After the so-called big change, they would probably just revert to their usual ruts."

Instead, a student who seldom left her desk adjusts her daily routine by taking a walk each morning and notices how this improves her depression symptoms. Another begins to consciously thank people during routine interactions and finds herself breaking the bad habits she has fallen into in her relationships with others. Or a talented basketball player takes up yoga to improve his game and discovers that it shifts his patterns on the basketball court and in other areas of his life, too.

"It's these seemingly small changes in their daily lives that add up to significant changes down the road," Puett explains.

Similarly, if we want to make changes in specific relationships, it helps to start small. For example, instead of diving into a big heart-to-heart with a difficult co-worker and expecting this to solve issues (and giving up on the situation if it doesn't), just start saying hello to him in the morning. Or offer to get him a cup of coffee on the next caffeine run. These small acts of kindness ease tension and build trust — this way, if and when you do have that heart-to-heart, it's much more likely to create positive change.

Little efforts like this are so important because we can control them. The world is changing constantly. Our best plans are often laid to waste simply because circumstances shift: we get jobs. We lose them. We get sick. We get well. We don't strictly control these events, but we can influence how we experience them by attending to the details that move us forward.

"Just as the world is not stable, [our] interactions are not fixed," Puett writes.

We don't need to move mountains to change our lives or heal our relationships. We just need to climb them, one step at a time.

Try It at Home: Start Small

Want to learn to cook? Start by focusing on three basic foods. If you can develop enough confidence to make eggs, a soup, and a salad, other things will feel less intimidating.

Want to start exercising? Begin with a short walk each morning. You'll get used to having a physical routine, which makes it more likely you'll stay committed when you buy a gym membership.

Want to fix a problem with your spouse? Before you sit down for that big heart-to-heart, restore your connection and build trust with some kind gestures. You'll have fewer walls to break down when you do talk.

Failure Is an Option

"I'm just not good at languages," the young woman says, blushing, as feelings of ineptitude wash over her. "I'm hopeless."

"There's no such thing," her Italian teacher encourages. "Try again."

Nearby, another student raises his hand. When the teacher nods, he launches into his own shaky Italian. Truthfully, the young woman realizes that it doesn't sound much better than hers. Yet, rather than blush and stammer, he smiles throughout, then listens without any trace of embarrassment as the teacher makes corrections.

The first student felt like a failure, while the other enjoyed the challenge and didn't take his mistakes personally or even think of them as mistakes. He saw them as learning opportunities. Again, the only difference is mindset.

A similar scenario inspired Carol Dweck, Ph.D., a psychology professor at Stanford University, to investigate the virtues of failure. Conducting a test with a group of children, she noticed that some actually seemed thrilled by their mistakes. "I love a challenge!" one boy said. Another,

Dweck notes in her book, "Mindset: The New Psychology of Success", was toiling away on some puzzles when he "looked up with a pleased expression and said with authority, <<You know, I was hoping this would be informative!>>".

At first, Dweck wondered what was wrong with them; she'd always thought of failure as something you just coped with. Then she became intrigued, which led her to explore the theory of "fixed" and "growth" mindsets.

Those with fixed mindsets believe their abilities are static traits — they have a certain capacity for something and that's that. They're good at languages or they're not. They're great athletes or they're not. A fixed mindset makes it difficult to leave our comfort zones or take risks; we're afraid setbacks will reflect poorly on us. In this state of mind, we take failures personally.

By contrast, people with a growth mindset perceive talents and abilities as something they can develop over time, through effort and instruction. They actively seek challenges, learn from mistakes, and persevere. They ask for help. They don't worry about appearing smart or talented, because they're more interested in learning and developing new skills.

These mindsets don't just affect us. They can have a profound influence on those around us — a fact that's especially relevant for managers, mentors, and teachers. A 2012 study in the Journal of Experimental Social Psychology found that a "fixed theory of math intelligence" can lead to a teacher diagnosing a student from just one test score. A low math-ability assessment often means teachers will offer less encouragement and assign less homework to the student, locking him or her into a cycle of low achievement.

Fortunately, and not surprisingly, a growth mindset is something we can develop.

Shifting toward a growth mindset begins with changing how we speak to ourselves. "If you hear that fixed-mindset voice in your head telling you not to take a risk, to pull out when you make a mistake start noticing that," Dweck advises.

"And then tell yourself, It's just the fixed-mindset voice in your head. And start answering back with a growth-mindset voice: You won't learn if you don't take the risk, and mistakes are OK."

Try It at Home: Stretch Yourself

The next time you miss the mark (the presentation bombs, the cake burns, you lose the game), instead of using all your mental energy to berate yourself, examine what happened. Try to identify three things you can do differently in the future.

Learn a completely new skill, one that you're not sure you can master. Focus on the learning process rather than the outcome. Even if you can't excel at this skill, what else can you gain from the experience?

Whenever you're afraid to ask for help because you feel like you should know something already, ask anyway.

Love Is Everywhere

The search for true love can, for some, be a never-ending quest. But what if someone told you that you've already found it and it's available all the time? With anyone you happen to encounter?

"Love is not a category of relationships. Nor is it something <<out there>> that you can fall into, or years later out of," explains Barbara Fredrickson, Ph.D., in her book, "Love 2.0.". "Love blossoms virtually anytime two or more people even strangers connect over a shared positive emotion."

Fredrickson, who teaches in the psychology department at the University of North Carolina, Chapel Hill, calls these moments of connection "positivity resonance". This expansive, science-based approach to love offers us many chances to experience it in the course of a single day. While it's not easy to set aside the Western idea that true love must be exclusive, lasting, and intimate, we have a lot to gain by letting it go.

That 90-second conversation you had with the stranger this morning while walking your dog? If there was eye contact, a sense of connection, and mutual respect — that's love. Whenever we exchange smiles or friendly gestures with strangers, or take a little extra time to have warm exchanges with people we see every day, those "micro-moments of positivity" change us at the biological level.

Princeton University neuroscientist Uri Hasson, Ph.D., a pioneer in neural mirroring (also known as "brain coupling"), examined brain scans of subjects in conversation. What he found was surprising, Fredrickson writes.

"Far from being isolated to one or two brain areas, really clicking with someone else appears to be a whole brain dance in a fully mirrored room." In good communication, she continues, "two individuals come to feel a single, shared emotion . . . distributed across their two brains."

The vagus nerve is also involved in forging personal connections. It stimulates the facial muscles necessary for making eye contact and synchronizing our expressions with others; it even helps the tiny muscles in the inner ear better track another voice amid background noise. We appear to be programmed to harmonize with fellow humans.

Micro-moments of positivity resonance also improve our health, she notes. "–People who experience more caring connections with others have fewer colds and lower blood pressure, and they less often succumb to heart disease and stroke, diabetes, Alzheimer's disease, and some cancers."

Much of Fredrickson's positivity research grew out of her study of loving-kindness meditation. This technique involves focusing on feelings of love, compassion and goodwill toward both yourself and others. It

"condition[s] your heart to be more open," she writes.

And when our hearts are open, love happens. All day. Every day.

Steven Mcryan

Try It at Home: Find Love

Make it a habit to look at people's faces — at the coffee shop, the dog park, the department store. You'll be more available to exchange a smile or a few friendly words.

Hold doors open for others when you get the chance.

Search for micro-moments with your family. Sit on the porch for a few minutes before bed; get up a little earlier so you can have breakfast together; call your sweetheart at lunch. All of these tiny gestures will add up to a great result.

CHAPTER 10

GROWTH MINDSET PARENTING

Research shows that parents can have a powerful impact on their children's mindsets. The language you use and the actions you make show your children what you expect. Giving praise during the process, talking about the brain, accepting mistakes as learning opportunities, and understanding the role of emotions in learning are all practices you can begin today.

The Importance of Praise

As parents, we all know the importance of praising our kids to encourage and condition them to bring out their best. In fact, studies suggest that it takes approximately five instances of genuine praise to balance the negativity of one instance of criticism. New research has found that there is most definitely a right and wrong way to praise kids, which can have drastic impacts on their learning potential, their performance and their motivation. In fact, it can all come down to one simple sentence that makes all the difference.

Fixed Mindset vs Growth Mindset

In a series of studies among school students, researchers wanted to temporarily induce either a "fixed mindset" or a "grown mindset" in children, and see what impact it would have on their academic performance.

A fixed mindset, by the way, is the assumption that people are either naturally good at something or they are not. A growth mindset, however, is the assumption that people who have achieved well at something did so because of the hard work and practice they put in.

So, in the most famous study, 5th graders were asked to individually complete a set of puzzle-based tests that the researchers knew the children would feel engaged with and perform well on. Each student was then taken aside, told that they achieved high marks and given praise for it. Half the group was randomly assigned to receive fixed-mindset praise, however, whilst the other half received growth-mindset praise. Before I tell you what the difference in praise was, firstly consider the implications of the results they found.

The Impact

After either praise was given, each child was told that because they did really well in the first test, they had the option to take an even more challenging test if they wanted to. They were also given the option of taking on some additional work so they can practise more at home to get even better. The kids in the growth mindset group were much more likely to decide to push themselves into the harder test and opt to practise more at home.

The other difference they found was that, even though all the kids in both groups said that they had enjoyed the original test, after the praise was given, the fixed mindset kids quickly stopped liking the whole process, whereas the growth mindset kids showed more enthusiasm and drive to continue throughout the follow-up tests, irrespective of how well they performed.

Then, at the end of all the testing, the researchers gave each student the original test they started with, and found that the fixed mindset kids actually performed worse on average than they had done the first time round

This research was not just one study either. It has been replicated in many different environments, at different ages, and has shown consistent results for over 30 years. The conclusion is that a fixed mindset created self-imposed restrictions on a learner's performance, whereas a growth mindset was clearly an important key to success.

How Parents Make The Biggest Difference

Fixed mindsets are incredibly common among our society. As parents who believe in the value of private tutoring, however, we know that hard work, effort and motivation can make all the difference. What many parents fall into the trap of doing, however, is accidentally creating a fixed mindset in the way theygive praise.

Growth Mindset In Kids

A child with a growth mindset will persist with tasks that are challenging and will not give up easily. They understand that the more effort they put into learning, the faster and smarter they get. They have a positive attitude towards challenges, because they know that even if they make mistakes when they try something new, that's how their brain learns and grows!

A Fixed Mindset In Kids

Someone with a fixed mindset sees their intelligence and abilities as unchangeable in spite of any effort.

Kids with fixed mindsets get stuck in the belief that they either have or do not have the abilities or smarts to do certain tasks. They tend to see things in black and white terms. Abject failure or absolute success. As a result, they give up easily when tasks get hard and beat themselves up for their mistakes and failures.

A Starting Point For Growth Mindset Parenting

The best we can do as parents is to become aware of the mindsets we nourish both in ourselves and our children. That way, we can monitor them and try to model and influence a growth mindset.

Sounds easy enough, but how do you actually do it? Can we actually change how our kids think? I definitely think so.

The Growth Mindset Parenting Self-Assessment

Now, when I say this is an informal self-assessment, what I mean is that it's a chance for you to think about some common parenting situations and how you typically respond to them.

There are no right or wrong answers here, and definitely no judgment!

"PARENTAL MOMENTS

There are definitely times in your daily routine that can serve as the perfect moments to help shape a growth mindset. In the education world, we call these "teachable moments".

The purpose of this reflection is to become more aware of these "teachable", or rather "parentable moments".

Once you start to recognize these moments, you can consciously observe both how your child reacts in these situations, and how you usually respond.

The more aware you become of how you are interacting with your child during these times, the easier it will be to use these opportunities to actively model growth mindset skills.

What To Say and What Not To Say

The way we praise our children can have a profound impact on their mindset. Research on praise and mindsets shows that when we praise children for being smart, this promotes a fixed mindset. It sends a message that their accomplishments are trait-based, and tied to something innate. In contrast, praising kids for working hard promotes a growth mindset. It sends a message that the child's effort is what led them to success. Want more tips on what to say and what not to say when praising your kids? Say this, not that!

- ➢ Say "I can see you have worked so hard on this!" Not "You are so smart!"

- Say "It seems like it's time to try a new strategy." Not "It's okay. Maybe you're just not cut out for this!"

- Say "I like watching you do that." Not "You're a natural at that!"

- Say "It looks like that was too easy for you. Let's find you something challenging so your brain can grow." Not "That's right! You did that so quickly and easily; great job!"

- Say "That's not right. You don't understand this yet. What strategies can you try to understand it better?" Not "That's not right. Are you paying attention in class? It seems like you're not even trying."

- Say "That was really hard. Your effort has paid off! Next time you'll be ready for this kind of challenge!" Not "That was really hard. I'm so glad it's over and you don't have to do that again."

- Say "You've worked hard to become a good writer. You should challenge yourself with an advanced class, and learn something you don't know how to do yet." Not "You have a real talent for writing. You should take a creative writing class because you're so good at it."

Talk About the Brain

The brain is far more malleable than we once thought. Teaching our kids that they actually have control over the way their brans grow through the actions they opt for is empowering! Tell your children that when they work hard, that's the feeling of their neurons connecting. The dendrites are reaching out to other dendrites, trying to connect to make a stronger brain. What strengthens those connections is practice, asking questions, and actively participating in learning. When children learn that their brains physically change with effort, this leads to increased motivation and achievement.

Accept Mistakes as Learning Opportunities

One of the best ways you can model a growth mindset is to speak candidly about the mistakes you've made and what you've learned from them. Speak positively about your mistakes and struggles, and this will show your children that taking risks and making mistakes are a natural part of the learning process. Explain to your children that trying hard things is what helps us grow, and you can't be perfect when you try something hard!

Understand the Role of Emotions in Learning

When we get angry, scared, or feel threatened, our fight or flight response is activated. This can happen anytime, whether we're scared of a spider or scared of math! Our brains are wired to protect us when we feel threatened, and stress symptoms such as sweating, stomach cramps, and our mind going blank are completely normal. There are strategies we can use when the fight or flight response tries to take over, to help us learn. One of those strategies is called Square Breathing, and it helps to break down the adrenaline that is flooding the bloodstream and preventing learning from occurring.

How to Criticize Kids Constructively

Criticism is one word that surely makes you raise your eyebrows and sulk. Arguably, it has no positive connotation for most of us. So, it is never received in a healthy way either. In this case, the matter of concern is, when we as adults can't handle criticism, what about the kids, who are subject to severe and regular criticism? Everybody who is somebody in their life comments and takes the liberty to pass judgement on their each and every act, most of which is, unfortunately, in critical form.

So, how to safeguard them or how to prepare them so that this unwarranted criticism does more good than harm to them? Criticism, sometimes called feedback, can be both constructive and destructive. Receiving feedback is a skill, and like most skills, it requires practice and a willingness to change and improve. Most children get plenty of practice. Ironically, adults need to help them make that practice count - namely by giving them feedback on how they handle criticism.

Feedback - both positive and negative - is challenging because it hits us in the vulnerable soft spot between our desire to grow and our deep need to be accepted and respected. The key to take feedback in a positive manner is to adopt a "growth mindset". People with a growth mindset believe that effort and challenge make us better, stronger and smarter, while those with a "fixed mindset" believe that our inherent assets are static no matter what we do.

But not all of the criticism kids face is constructive. Some of it is born out of ulterior motives or dark intentions; however, the good news is that a growth mindset can protect kids from this sort of feedback as well.

A growth mindset is the best gift we can give to our children. Thus armed, they can be brave in the face of constructive criticism, believing it can make them better, stronger and smarter. They won't need us to safeguard their interest because, given a growth mindset, kids can handle the truth all by themselves.

So, what to do?

- ➤ ***Don't hesitate to criticize:*** Many kids have trouble hearing feedback because they don't experience it often enough. While it's natural to want to protect children from pain, when we protect our kids from criticism or focus excessively on praise, we push them toward a fixed mindset.

- ➤ ***Stop constant praise:*** An effusive praise may encourage a fixed mindset and consequently discourage children from taking on new challenges. Worse, it can deflate, rather than shore up, self-esteem in some kids. Children need to get used to hearing constructive feedback, and it's our job to teach them how.

- ➤ ***Mind your body language:*** Non-verbal communication is part of delivering feedback, and can help kids hear it more effectively. Uncross your arms, get down on the kids' level, smile and keep your face relaxed. If you are tense when you hand out criticism, they will be tense when they receive it.

- ➤ ***Switch up your pronouns:*** Instead of framing feedback in terms of "I'm so proud of you", turn the statement and anchor feedback in the pronoun "you," as in, "You should be proud of yourself," or "What did you feel best about?" or "What one thing would you like to change?"

- ➤ ***Empower for change:*** Lessen your control and hand power over to the children, helping them adjust their efforts to use feedback effectively. Ask, "Is that how you'd hoped this would turn out?" or "What would you do differently the next time?". Help them see the way forward with comments like, "How do you think you could take this project from good to awesome?"

- ➤ ***Set new goals after a big failure:*** Once they have picked themselves up, help them pick some new goals based on what they have learned from the situation at hand. Their goals should be their own, devised by them, based on their experience.

Criticism comes to everyone, eventually. It's inescapable, and more relevantly, it's a necessary part of growing up. As we can't protect children from it, the best we can do is ensure that they are equipped with the emotional fortitude and strength of character they will need to forge ahead, stronger, smarter and braver for the experience.

What Helps Children Become Confident and Successful Learners?

Enthusiasm is a great start, and research suggests it is a sign of future success. When children start school they are often told to sit quietly and listen to the teacher, but children who shouted out answers in class turned out to be the most successful learners as they progressed through school. Our common sense tells us this research is only a partial truth. The story made good headlines because it challenged popular opinion. But what really does make children more confident and effective in school?

The research completed by a team at Durham University looked specifically at 4 and 5-year-olds in their first year at school. The team collected data about 12,000 children from teachers in over 500 schools. Now, children at this age are new to the techniques of working in a busy classroom, and teachers have only just started to instil classroom discipline. Little ones do tend to blurt things out and get carried away. It's what young children do. The ones at the back keeping quiet were not necessarily polite. This group would include those who just didn't know the answer and were waiting to be told everything.

To suggest that calling out is a useful indicator of potential to succeed at any age is beyond the remit of the research. What I think the research is saying, is that at this age, you can tell who is knowledgeable, motivated and engaged because they participate, albeit ineptly, by shouting over each other and not giving those who need more thinking time a look in. We would expect nothing else at this age. Keen and green. Later, children learn to take turns, share, and pay attention to others. Right now, though, they haven't got the emotional or cognitive abilities to see the world from any perspective other than their own. They don't know any different. So in the longer term, what is the evidence on how to help children become motivated and skilled learners? Here are 7 factors which help a child succeed.

The ability to focus attention and avoid distraction is a major factor in the long run. You take less in and get less done if you are poor at paying attention.

Play is important, it helps children practice planning, thinking and carrying things through to completion. Learning to restrain impulsiveness is vital.

Emotional wellbeing has a big impact on learning. Children need security and nurturing to be able to shift their focus of attention beyond their own needs.

IQ or ability do count, but they are not as strongly predictive of success as people assume. Ability needs to be put to good use, and this may not happen if children have poor concentration or are distracted by insecurity.

A growth mindset is more important than ability. A child who focuses on putting effort in will get results. The child who sees learning ability as a muscle which strengthens with practice will keep going, while the child who believes in a fixed ability will cave in when the going gets tough.

A well developed vocabulary is vital for both understanding and sharing what you are learning. This is highly associated with "parents who listen so children can talk". Rather than specifically teaching vocabulary, responsiveness from adults appears to be the key. Positive communication allows a child to explore and learn – with adult support.

Children need to work to their strengths. Children sustain their interest in and effort with topics which are real and relevant to them. They need to be fully associated with what they learn in primary school, and can't yet take the impartial detached position which the academic analysis of a subject requires.

CHAPTER 11

THE LAW OF ATTRACTION WITH CHANGING ONE'S MINDSET

The Law of Attraction says that what we focus on is what we attract. Now, please understand that this has nothing to do with emotions, but everything to do with your thoughts.

"Your thoughts are the architects of your destiny." - David O. McKay

Stumbling upon this quote really opened my eyes to how the way that we think can play a part in determining our actions. We block our blessings when we continuously invest our time in thinking negatively. If we are really aiming to achieve the best life possible, we have to change our line of thinking!

The History Of The Law Of Attraction

Before you embark on the incredible journey towards true enlightenment in the Law of Attraction, it is important that you understand that you can apply it to your life and it can be effective only if the correct tools are used. The practices and beliefs in this law have been igniting the lives of great individuals throughout the course of history.

Hundreds of years ago, the Law of Attraction was first thought to have been taught to man by the immortal Buddha. It is believed he wanted it to be known that "what you have become is what you have thought". This is a belief that is deeply intrinsic in the Law of Attraction.

With the spread of this concept to Western culture, the term "Karma" also came about. Karma is now a popular a belief in numerous societies.

Over the centuries it has been a common understanding amongst many that what you give out to the world (be it anger or happiness, hate or love) is ultimately what will return to your own life in the end. This simple and easy-to-follow concept has been extremely popular among many for a quite a number of years. It demonstrates that the idea behind the power of attraction is not new whatsoever. It is already recognizable to many of us in a variety of forms.

The main principles of the Law of Attraction can also be discovered in the teachings of many civilizations and religious groups. An example: in the Proverbs 23:7, it reads, "As a man thinketh in his heart so is he". Proof of praise for the Laws of Attraction can be uncovered throughout the ages; all recorded and taught in different ways, but still there for all of humanity to find.

Is The Law Of Attraction Real?

As previously discussed, The Law Of Attraction and its values have surfaced many times throughout history. And a great many women and men who have left their mark on this world have shown the Law of Attraction to be one of the greatest powers on Earth, with many well-loved poets, artists, scientists and great thinkers such as Shakespeare, Blake, Emerson, Newton and Beethoven all conveying this message through their many works.

There have been many modern advocates of The Law Of Attraction as well. These include Oprah Winfrey, Jim Carrey, and Denzel Washington. In addition, with over 5.8 MILLION Facebook fans, there are plenty of success stories surrounding The Law Of Attraction.

The most challenging part of acknowledging and accepting the truth of what the Law of Attraction has to offer is coming to the realization that every single one of your decisions in life, good and bad, have been shaped by you alone. For many, this can be a bitter pill to swallow, especially if you feel that you or your loved ones have been dealt some particularly hard blows in life.

However, once you have truly come to understand the true key behind of the Law of Attraction you can be filled with renewed hope and courage in the overwhelming knowledge that you are free to take charge of your life and forever free yourself from the cycle of fear, worry or negativity which has held you back for too long.

The Science Behind The Law Of Attraction: Fact, Not Fiction

In recent years, the work of quantum physicists has helped to cast greater light on the incredible impact that the power of the mind has on our lives and the universe in general. The more this idea is explored by scientists and great thinkers alike, the greater an understanding we have on just how significant a role the mind plays in shaping our lives and the world around us.

It doesn't matter if you do not ever come to have a thorough understanding of the quantum physics behind the Law of Attraction. However, this does not mean that we all cannot enjoy the many benefits that this generous law can offer us. As physicists come to supply us with more and more information regarding the law, the more we can simply rejoice in the truly liberating and empowering realization that we are the creators and controllers of our life and the energy we are all made of.

Be happy, for the universe is always on our side! The more time you dedicate to learning how to use the Law of Attraction effectively, the more fulfilling and rewarding your life can be. There are no restrictions! Open your mind and enjoy the natural abundance of the Universe.

How To Use The Law Of Attraction

Once we have come to understand the astounding possibilities that life has to offer, we can also come to realize that we are like artists. We are creating pictures of our intended life and then making choices and taking actions that will realize what we have envisaged.

So, what if you don't like the picture? Change it!

Life is a blank canvas of possibility; you are in control of what the finished picture could look like.

The Law of Attraction really is that simple. No catches. All the laws of nature are completely perfect and the Law of Attraction is no exception. No matter what you are looking to have, achieve or be in life, if you can hold onto an idea and see it for yourself with your mind's eye, you can make it yours to have… with some effort on your part, of course.

Why The Law Of Attraction Works

How the Law of Attraction works can be explained in many ways, but the two most common schools of thought are:

- ❖ *The Spiritual Explanation:* Many people tend to think that the Law of Attraction is when they affiliate their goals with God or the Universe. They also believe that, because they are made up of energy on different frequencies, they can alter their frequency by indulging in positive thoughts. With the use of positive thoughts and by aligning these with their goals instead of dwelling on the negatives, they are certain that the Law of Attraction will "walk in" with a whole bundle of positivity. The key, though, is to believe that what they seek is already theirs, or it will be soon.

- ❖ *The Scientific Explanation:* For those of you who do not fancy the spiritual, this explanation may appease you. When you have changed your thought process and start thinking positively, you begin to take more risks and bare yourself to new possibilities. For example, you may want to achieve a certain goal, so you put yourself out there to be more accessible to achieve said goal. On the other hand, when you do not believe that something is in line for you, oftentimes you let those opportunities pass you by.

Manifesting Your Dreams

Most times people want their dreams to become a reality, but what they do not understand is that they must have their thoughts in alignment with the said dream. A positive mindset is key when achieving your goals, as this will attract positive energy to you. However, please bear in mind that this is something that you will have to work extremely hard to achieve. Your brain stores a lot of your fears, hurt, and pain previously experienced, and these won't just go away after one positive thought. You will have to rewire your brain by applying certain practices to train it into thinking positively.

Below are three practices you can adopt to help manifest greatness in your lives:

Be careful of what you focus on: Instead of focusing all your energy on things that are going wrong, think about all the things that are going right. In life, obstacles and shortcomings will come at you hard and fast, but it is your duty to focus on the positives of the situation. When you develop a positive mindset, you will realize that your problem-solving skills and your confidence will improve.

Write! Write! Write!: When I am worried or stressed, the quickest thing I do is grab a book and a pen (which is always on hand, btw) and start writing. I write everything that is frustrating me in the form of a list. This gives me a form of visual representation that not only makes things easier for me to work out, but also releases some of the built-up energy that I have stored. This method really helps especially when I am too frustrated to talk to anyone. I just write down my frustrations and hand the book to my mother, like "Mummy, here. I cannot talk right now but this is what is stressing me out." Man, this is my favorite method, it helps!

Write down your goals and think of how you will feel when they have come to pass. Not only will this push you in a positive direction, but it will also propel you into positive situations and cause people to enter your life that will help you to get to where you need to be.

Envision your dreams: When? In the mornings, right after you have woken up, and at nights, before you go to bed, read the goals that you have written. This will allow you to form a connection with them and allow them to manifest within the universe.

Assess yourself to see if you lean more towards the pessimistic or the optimistic side of life. With this knowledge, you will know what you need to do to achieve your goals – whether you need to add some daily affirmations into your daily schedule or you just need to continue what you were doing because you're doing great, sweetie. Your destiny is in your hands; it is up to you to make the right decision for you!

CONCLUSION

In order to achieve your goals, your mindset needs to match your aspirations; otherwise, it might be holding you back from getting where you want to be.

Here are 7 effective ways to upgrade your mindset:

1. *Change your Self-Talk:* The conversations you have with yourself are a direct reflection of your mindset. If you are telling yourself, "I am not good enough to achieve my dreams", your thoughts will create your reality and your mindset will hold you back from having the life you want. To upgrade your mindset, change your negative self-talk to an empowerment speech. Sounds cliché, but telling yourself "I can do this" or "I got this" really works.

2. *Change your Language:* After changing your inner thought dialogue and the story you are telling yourself, change the way you talk to other people. Avoid phrases like "I am always like this" or "I am always doing this" in order to encourage a growth mindset instead. Furthermore, make it a habit to talk about the things that are going well in your life instead of complaining and

talking about your problems. This will encourage a mindset of abundance instead of fear and shortcomings.

3. ***Determine the mindset you need and act as if:*** Pick a goal you want to achieve and ask yourself: *"Which mindset do I need to achieve this goal?"* and *"Which mindset do people have that have already been successful at this goal?"*.

4. For example, healthy and fit people might share the mindset "I love taking care of my body, nourishing it with whole foods and exercising every day". If it's your goal to be healthy and fit, act as if you already HAVE the mindset of a healthy and fit person. This way, you are basically tricking your brain into adopting a new mindset and reinforcing it with action.

5. ***Learn & Apply:*** Read books from great minds to understand and adopt their thinking. Read books about how the mind and brain work. Learn from mindset experts through online courses, events, and coaching.

Here are some of my favorite mindset resources:

a. "Mindset" by Carol Dweck - to learn about the growth mindset

b. "Everything" from Gabrielle Bernstein - to adopt a mindset of abundance and align with the flow of life

c. The writing of Thomas Oppong, "Medium for great nuggets" - on improving your thinking

d. The Online Courses from Denise DT for upgrading your money mindset

Open Mindset

6. **Surround yourself with people that match your desired mindset:** Want to upgrade your money and success mindset? Start hanging out with people that are very successful and seem to have an abundance of money flowing their way at any time. It is easier to adopt a new mindset when you see that it is already working for other people. Learn how they think and adapt their daily habits to match their mindset.

7. **Create new habits to support your mindset change:** Integrate powerful habits into your day that help your mindset change and reenforce your thinking with action. If you are upgrading from "fixed" to "growth" mindset, schedule time for learning and start noting down your learnings and achievements every day. If you are upgrading from a

8. "destination" to "journey" mindset, practice being mindful, enjoying the present moment and celebrating small successes.

9. **Jump out of your comfort zone:** If you put yourself in situations that challenge you, you have no other choice than to rise to the occasion and upgrade your mindset. It becomes a necessity to survive.

So, ask yourself "What situations can I put myself in that will require me to operate on a higher mindset?". Basically, the idea is to engineer your environment to train your brain!

DISCLAIMER

All the material contained in this book is provided for educational and informational purposes only. No responsibility can be taken for any results or outcomes resulting from the use of this material. While every attempt has been made to provide information that is both accurate and effective, the author does not assume any responsibility for the accuracy or use/misuse of this information.